THE MYSTERY IS UNLOCKED

What happens when a person Dies

Daniel Elijah Joseph

ISBN: 978-1-8380375-3-6
        978-1-8380375-4-3
        978-1-8380375-5-0

CONTENTS

INTRODUCTION

 *It is not good for a soul to be without knowledge. (Prov. 19:2a) And it shall come to pass in the last days, says God … I will show wonders in heaven above. (Acts 2:17-19)*

Every group of people has different concepts and beliefs about the afterlife. Various religions also have different beliefs. That is fine, and my motto is to each his own. One thing that I believe with all my heart is that there is only one truth. We may have different interpretations of

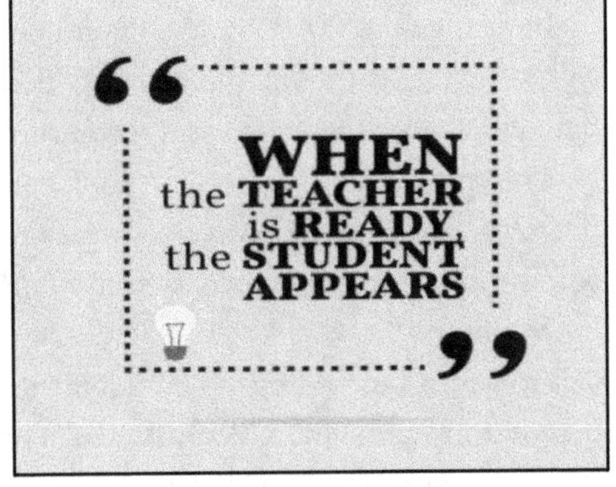

the truth, but the fact remains that there is one truth. This piece of literature is about finding out what some religions and spiritual groups think about the human soul, and the places we go when we leave this time and space reality.

It's important that we take ownership of our souls, and that we know what is likely to happen to them when they leave our physical bodies. Our actions and attitude have a large impact on our souls' next destination in the spirit realm. We prepare and plan for a lot of things in our world, such as holidays, careers, and family. Doesn't it make sense that we understand the reason why we came and the significance of our actions and attitudes? Then we can ultimately influence the place we go in the afterlife, and when we have such a mind-set, we make our world a better place.

The Mystery Is UNLOCKED – What happens to a person when they die?

We are still early in the year 2020, and at the beginning of the year, one might have felt 2020 would be a great year, especially with the numbers 2020: perfect eyesight, so perhaps perfect year.

Unfortunately, the first quarter of the year has shown no sign of year 2020 being a perfect or even a good year for a lot of people. Many have lost loved ones from the coronavirus (COVID-19) that originated in China last year.

In as much as 2020 could still end up being a great year, I am sure you will all agree with me that so far, the sorrow of death has hit many families all over the world as a result of the coronavirus pandemic.

This pandemic is affecting all facets of life, from education to the financial markets, and travel as cities are on lockdown. The world has come to a standstill, which is something we have never experienced on Earth before.

However, according to Wikipedia, the **1889–1890 flu pandemic**, better known as the **"Asiatic flu"** or **"Russian flu,"** was a deadly influenza pandemic that killed about 1 million people worldwide. It was the last great pandemic of the 19th century.

The question on everybody's mine is, when is this pandemic going to come to an end, so we can have our normal lives back?

Another important question is, what does all this mean? The answer to that question depends on one's perception of life. Personally, I have a spiritual mindset; therefore, I compare events in the world with what's written in the Bible, and I must say it feels like the written word of God is being fulfilled in my lifetime.

In the Bible, the Book of Revelation calls this period a time of trial for the whole world. It's also appropriate to says this is a time of God's judgement.

Hence, it's important that we pray and ask God for His mercy on the whole world, but it's fair to say this coronavirus has forever changed our lives.

No one really knows the ultimate impact this virus will have on people, but one thing is for sure: things may never be as they used to be.

Do not get me wrong: I am not for a second saying that we should live in fear of death, but the opposite. We should have faith that we continue our journey in the spirit realm and that the decisions we make while here are crucial.

Emphasis will be placed a lot on my faith, which is Christianity, but I will look into what other religions and spiritual groups have to say in regards to the human soul, reincarnation, and our final destinations.

After watching two TV programmes, the movie *Prophecy* and the TV series *Once Upon a Time*, I started to ponder on the human soul because it played a key part in both of these programmes. They are both fiction, but I know that there is a lot of spiritual truth in both of them. *Prophecy* (written by Gregory Widen and starring Christopher Walken) has three parts and was about a general who had died, but during his lifetime, he sold his soul to the dark side. Upon his death, the Devil came to collect what was his.

In the American TV Series called *Once Upon a Time*.

There were incidents where people desired a blessing or something special, and they would go to a particular individual who possessed dark magic to grant their request. However, they always had to pay a price, which was usually something very dear to them, and most of the time it was a person; basically, a person would be the sacrifice.

I have heard things like this happen a lot in our society, and living in Africa for many years opened my eyes more clearly to the world of witchcraft and dark magic. There are also a lot of clips on YouTube about such related topics. The question is, are these stories true? Such topics are not the average conversations people have; it's kind of like an underground conversation. The problem with that is that people could be deceived and then act in ignorance. The sad thing is whether or not there's ignorance, the consequence of a person's actions will have to be paid, especially when it relates to spiritual matters. A verse that comes to mind is Hosea 4:6 – 'My people perish from lack of knowledge.' The *Oxford Dictionary* defines *perish* as 'suffer death, typically in a violent, sudden or untimely way'.

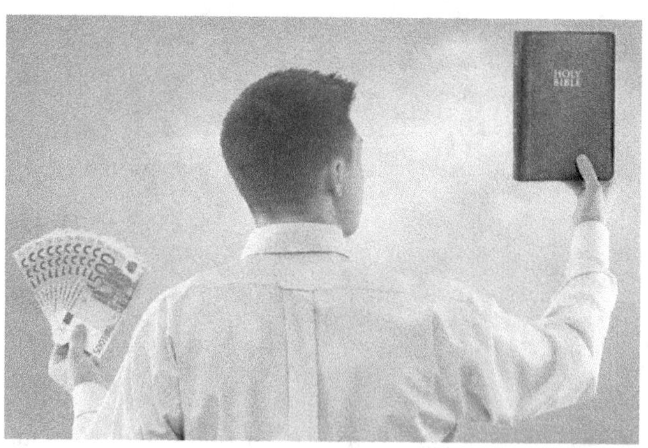

The very nature of God is that He gives us all free will. God never forces us to do anything – the choice is ours. However, from my experience of living in our world and observing human interaction and behaviour, some people are manipulated into believing a lie (sometimes by means of enchantments, or witchcraft) and undertaking an action for which they then have to pay a heavy price. The consequence could ultimately be the place they spend eternity.

We have heard a lot of stories and rumours of people suffering and perishing in some way, and for the most part, we take it lightly and never really ponder the reasons behind the incidents or tragedies.

This is what people fail to realise: the spirit world is the most powerful world, and it controls this our natural world. Every act we engage in, especially that related to the supernatural or spirit world, has a consequence, whether good or bad. You sow what you reap cycle, and for every action there is a reaction. Another important thing to consider is that the repercussions are not limited to time and space (this physical world); they have eternal implications. This is what has led me to my research on the human soul, and why people sell it and transact it.

The teachings of Jesus talk a lot about the soul. For example, Mark 8:36–37 states, 'For what would it profit a man, if he shall gain the whole world, and lose his own soul? Or what shall a man give in exchange for his own soul? If we look at the amplified version of the same verses it could help us with more clarity … For what does it profit a man to gain the whole world, and forfeit his life [in the eternal kingdom of God]?' (AMP).

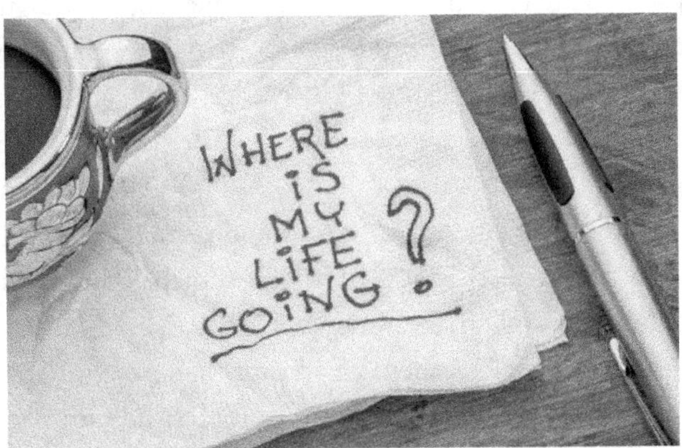

To lose something means one doesn't have ownership of it anymore; someone else does. The person or spirit that has ownership of the soul controls the soul, and ultimately controls the person.

Jesus also put it in another way: when riches and fame are given for the exchange of a soul, such a person will forfeit his or her place in the kingdom of God.

In order for an individual to not fall for this trap, that person must be able to see into the spirit world of God and set one's mind on things above, not below, our time and space reality.

That's how the quest began: to research what the human soul is all about. I believe there are other movies that also share the same theme of selling one's soul for the exchange of material goods or fame, and if I come across any more, I will watch them and give my opinion.

What I personally believe is that the soul lives forever; however, we determine where it lives. I also believe what we are given second chances to come down to time and space to make amends, correct situations, and redeem our soul.

I also have a feeling that only if, at a person's point of death, and one hasn't tried to make amends and to embrace the kingdom of light, then the soul could end up in a dark place for all eternity. I am also aware of the seven spheres, including the kingdom or spiritual sphere available to us in the afterlife.

The most important things in our lives – and existence itself – in this time and space reality are our human souls. They should be guarded with all of our might. As one gets more enlightened, we see it's more important than money, career accomplishments, and life itself. The reason for its importance is because I believe it qualifies us for our afterlife destination. There is a hierarchy in the spirit world, and depending on the accomplishment of our assignment, that will determine our rank and place in the non-physical world. That is why the topic of this book, which is around the human soul, makes me feel excited as I proceed on this journey. I have also been a student of spiritual literature insight for quite a while now, and based on my numerology life path number, I am not surprised. This is a new phrase in my life, and I am motivated and galvanized about writing on the topics that capture my interest. When I was young and in high school, I wasn't a fan of literature due to several reasons that I couldn't control at the time. However, as I have grown and matured, I can say I really appreciate art of all forms. Creativity makes me come alive, and it helps me answer some questions I have about life. I have found that writing as a form of creativity helps me transcend, and then I get insight to various aspects of life. I sometimes wonder why it took so long to come to this realisation of the benefits and importance of writing. My only conclusion would be that in order to be a writer, we need life experience, and we come to the place we can trust our thoughts and realise the moments when we are one with God and have the mind of God.

Don't get me wrong: I have done some form of writing in the past, when I was in college, studied accountancy, and had my dissertations for my MBA. However, this is what I call free will writing based on my experience from the university of life and beyond.

Every now and then, I enjoy stimulated conversations, but now I would like to put these conversations on paper and be a writer. I will cover areas that will help us the human race as a whole. Also, I like to refer to myself as a spiritual Christian, because I have seen a lot of people who do a lot of nasty things and then hide behind religion. In other words, *religion* is not my favourite word.

My writings now and in the future will comprise of psychology, sociology, neuroscience, and how they all link to our inner person, our spirit being. Therefore I will let the Holy Spirit lead me along this new phrase and journey of my life.

A known fact that all creative and artistic people will agree on is that any form of art or creativity, such as literature, helps us transcend to higher consciousness. To be honest, that is a place I always like to be. Going back to the topic at hand, I believe it's long overdue for some light to be shed on it. As we know and read in the Bible, people suffer for lack of knowledge, which means is that being ignorant is no excuse. What I really find interesting is that most holy books are coded, and we need a helping hand from a higher force to give us insight and revelation.

I have also found out that most people like things to be done for them. That is good in some instances, but when it comes to spiritual matters, you have to be 100 per cent careful. The reason is that you are given power to someone else, and that individual or group of individuals could manipulate you. This has been my experience, but it doesn't have to be yours. You might be more fortunate and have good people to guide you along your spiritual journey.

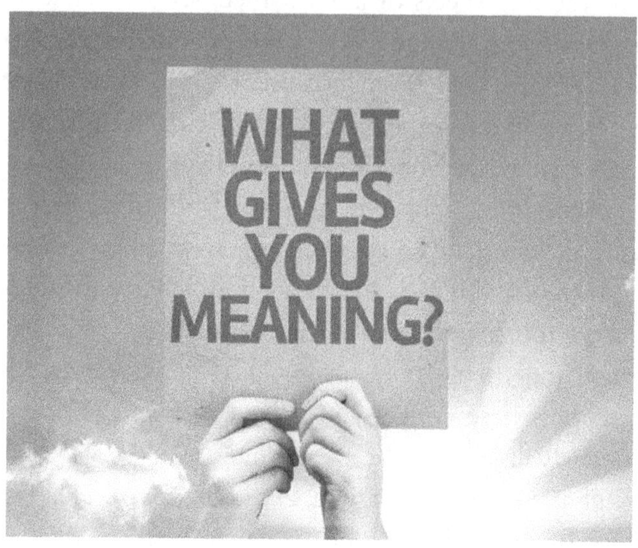

I look back now and am so thankful for my experiences, because they have enabled me to learn a lot of stuff about life, and money can't buy that. There is a famous quote that I really believe to be true in my life: 'Words don't teach; only life experiences teach' We can learn a little bit from some people, but ultimately we learn from the stuff we go through.

This topic of the human soul will cover what the main religions say about it. For those that don't really say much about it, I will be reading between the lines of main figures in the holy books. What I find interesting is that the same thing will happen to every soul under certain conditions, whether or not a religion talks about it.

I also believe that religious books contradict themselves, but I think that lies solely in the hands of humans. We all know that they were translated from an original text for the most part, and as a result, human error cannot be ruled out. Another important factor is when reading holy scriptures, one should ideally be in a higher consciousness. (A Christian would say 'being in the spirit,' but some would say being 'in the zone' or 'in the vortex,' **a phrase used by the new age movement.**) The whole point of this is that you are in a place where you can get insight and revelation. As I mentioned earlier, these books are coded, and you have to be able to read between the lines and decode what its saying. The good thing is that when you are in that state of higher consciousness, you have angels and the Holy Spirit with you, revealing truth and teaching you what you need to know at that point in time.

I believe people don't like addressing such topics as the human soul

is because they are afraid of death. I don't think we should be. If we have played our cards right, we will go to a much better place. However, if we think we are not playing our cards right, then we need to start addressing some aspects of our lives that need attention, which ultimately boils down to the four-letter word: *love*. We have to get our love walk right.

Speaking of love, I have come across some people who practice witchcraft, and to me they are wicked people; I wonder how they sleep at night. What they do to people is evil and is the opposite of love. The main reason why my spirituality will always be based on the Christian faith is because I have seen the love of God, Jesus, and the Holy Spirit. It hasn't equated in material means yet (humans look for evidence in materialism), but in the feelings of peace and joy.

Love is where it starts, and love is where it will end. Regardless of your religion or beliefs, they all say the same thing, which is that God is love. If we see ourselves acting in some areas that do not reflect the attitude of love, then with help from above, we should start to address those areas.

Once we start to do this and are true to ourselves, then the fear of death will cease to exist, and we can start to address things of this life and the afterlife. Just like taxes, we can't escape it. More important, it's our souls that bring about the continuation of our existence. As a friend of mine said to me some time ago, our being on the earth in this time and space is simply a blip of our existence.

Let's start addressing the important issues of our existence. I am not against material things, partners, and careers. What we should never forget is that each and every single one of us is on a spiritual pilgrimage, whether or not we know it. I sincerely believe that for the most part, people have forgotten about their real reasons for being here, and they've been lost in the rat race.

Chapter 1

WHAT IS THE HUMAN SOUL?

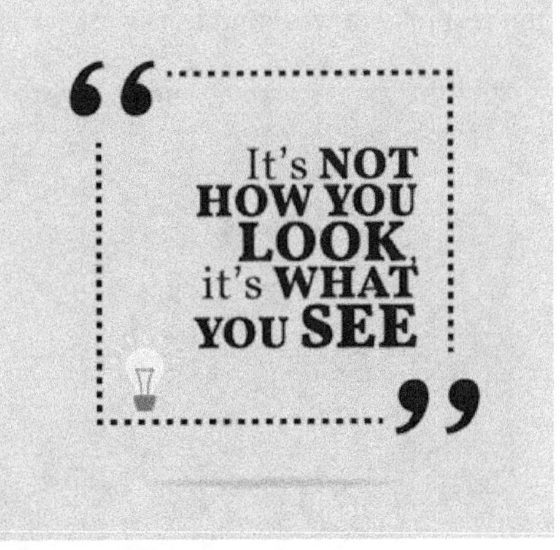

I will start by giving my definition of the human soul: a separate entity, independent of our physical body, that helps give life to the physical body. It is a true representation of who one really is. It existed before one was conceived in a mother's womb and will still exist after one dies. This part of a human is disembodied after death. The word *disembodied* means free from the body. And while we are talking about the human soul, it means to free the human soul from the body at the point of death.

Our souls existed before our bodies were formed, and they will continue to exist when our physical bodies are dead and gone. We are in physical bodies (containers), and when we go to the spirit world, we will have spiritual bodies. Our souls have to answer to what we did with our lives, which will lead to a promotion, demotion, or being at the same place we were before we came to this physical world. **The Bible says we will give an account for our life and a reward awaits those who have been faithful. Also in the Kingdom of God and in the spirit world in general, there are ranks. What I mean is, there is a hierarchy.**

The human can also be perceived as the connecting link to the spirit world. While we are still in the physical form, the soul can grow into something nice and beautiful – or nasty and bad.

When a soul enters a body, it gives life to the body; when it leaves the body, the body is dead. But the soul can never die. Even the souls that go to hell don't die; they are simply in damnation forever. The soul is such a powerful entity that can be felt by people. Some people's souls can be read straightaway, either good or bad. It could be a feeling vibration, or it could be written all over a person's face.

Our souls are much more than our physical appearance. They are the embodiment of who we really are and our essence, and they help reveal the real reason we came to this physical world.

Human beings exist in dual dimensions. We exist in the spiritual dimension and the physical dimension at the same time. When we sleep, we go to the spiritual dimension. We probably don't remember when we wake up. The apostle Paul got a revelation and said that Christians are seated with Christ in heavenly places. Christ is kind of like a title that means 'the anointed one', and His anointing means the power of God. Basically, a Christian is in the power of God and operates in two places:

the spirit world and the physical world. However, this is not automatic. For Christians to experience this, they have to be spiritually minded and not carnally minded. It can also be looked at as being in the spirit or being in the flesh. Being in the high place of consciousness takes discipline, and God is able to give us grace for it.

The soul of a person has been a topic of curiosity since time began. Most people of depth will ask, 'Why am I here? What is all this about? Where did we come from? And what happens when we die?' In spiritual and religious groups, the word *incorporeal* is used in helping to describe the human soul, and it means without physical body, presence, or form. God, the human spirit, and soul can be regarded as incorporeal. Also, the Abrahamic religions (Judaism, Christianity, and Islam) are the primary focus of my research because all try to answer the question of immortal essence of the souls of the human race.

According to Cross and Livingstone (1997), the Catholic theologian Thomas Aquinas ascribes a soul to all organisms, but only the human soul is immortal. It is even fair to say that the word *soul* has various meanings. My focus is on the human soul. The human soul grows and matures just as our physical bodies grow and mature.

Some other religions, such as Jainism and Hinduism, also hold the concept that everything, including living and nonliving things (from animals to rivers), has a soul. I do agree with this; however, I would rather use the word *energy*. Everything has energy. Everything vibrates, and we pick up vibrations of human and nonhuman beings.

The focus at hand is the human soul. Another word for the human soul is *anima*, which means an individual's true inner self. In his analytic psychology, C. G. Jung reflects the archetypal ideas of conduct – an inner feminine part of the male personality, and the part of the psyche that is directed inward and is in touch with the subconscious. This also includes the inner personality that is turned towards the unconscious of the individual (Jung 1968).

It's interesting that the inner self is described alongside the inner feminine part of the male personality. We have two sides in our brain, the left and the right sides. The left side is the logic part of the brain, which men tend to use the most. Females often use the right side of the brain. This right side is more of the spiritual side. Females are more touchy- feely individuals with strong intuition, and spiritual people tend to use the right side of the brain. Another way to put it is using your heart or your head. Again, most men use logic and reason, whereas women go for the feeling sense of things, which is key in understanding the spirit. Faith is linked to the right side of the brain too, because you can't use logic or reason to comprehend faith. Therefore, it's understandable how the human soul (anima) is described as the inner feminine part of man's personality.

Our souls' physical appearances can sometimes reflect our souls, but this is not always the case. The soul is our inner self or being. This could sometimes be revealed through a person's countenance, but in some instances it might be covered up. People are sometimes in disguise. Not to disrespect females, but a good example could be a female with and without make-up. The vibration could be different in these two instances. Finding the real inner personality would be via conversation and not appearance. A person might still be able to pick up the type of soul an individual has by appearance; however, there are chances that it could be wrong.

Our human souls encompass one mystery that needs to be resolved. As Aurelius (2004: 21) stated, 'Ignoring what goes on in other people's souls – no one ever came to grief that way. But if you won't keep track of what your own soul's doing, how can you not be unhappy?' To add to that, I say in order for me to keep track, I have to have a clear understanding of what my human soul really is, because I will always suffer the consequents of my ignorance, especially spiritual unawareness.

Marcus Aurelius was a Roman emperor from AD 161–180. He was classified as one of the so-called five good emperors. One would expect human consciousness to be in a much higher place than it is today. I personally think human consciousness has deteriorated over the years, and we are not in pursuit of what really matters. In this day and age, you can hardly find anyone who has an understanding of the soul and the actions to take to improve the soul. This indicates to me that humankind is in a dark place and that this darkness is overshadowing the light. I don't want to sound negative, but we need enlightenment like never before. People *must* be made aware of the fact that the practise of witchcraft or other wickedness has an impact on the human soul. I know people's hearts are hardened, but only God melts a hard heart. Also, God never imposes. It's all about free will. Having said that, the spiritual law that says people will always reap what they sow. This is law.

Even Greek philosophers such as Plato, Socrates, and Aristotle knew the importance of the human soul, and trying to understand it played a significant part of their works. The soul is our essence, and the mission and purpose is first determined before the human body is formed. Our essence is the important part of us; knowing our essence is crucial to knowing our mission and purpose.

Ropper (1966) notes that Plato believed that the soul is among the first of things – and prior to all bodies. I also share the above view as God told Jeremiah the prophet – 'I knew you before I formed you and sanctified you, before you were born' – which could only mean one thing: we existed before we were formed in the wombs of our mothers.

To Whom Do Our Souls Belong?

Let me start with 1Kings 17:21: 'O Lord my God, I pray You, let this child's soul come back into him.'

 The picture above shows Prophet Elijah raises the son of the widow of Zarephath from the dead.

And the Lord heard the voice of Elijah, and the soul of the child came into him again, and he revived. (1 Kings 17:22)

In the above instance, the boy's soul belonged to God. God took it and gave it back, maybe to accredit Elijah. After the child came back to life, his mother said, 'By this I know that you are a man of God and the word of the Lord in your mouth is truth.'

This other verse says *body*, but what we are trying to establish is this: who owns us when we die? Michael the archangel, when contending with the Devil, disputed about the body of Moses. I think the only reason this could happen was because Moses grew up as a child in the court of Pharaoh, and we know what they were involved in. As a child, Moses probably had all the (demonic) rituals done to him.

The point is this our souls go to the kingdom of light, the kingdom of darkness, or what I like to call default.

The definition of a soul is not complete until one mentions the powers and forces that govern our universe. We are all part of the universe, and we are obviously affected by these powers and forces.

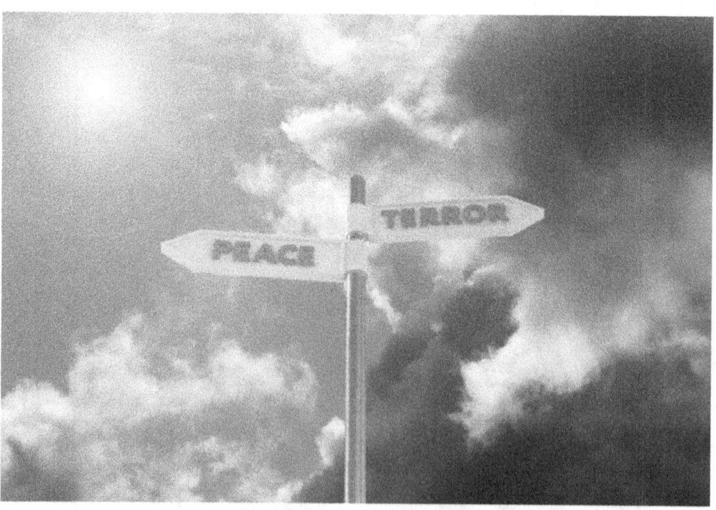

This can simply be put as light and darkness. Another way to put it is the kingdom of light and the kingdom of darkness, or good and bad. I believe that all religions think along this line.

Let's go back to the simple definition of *Merriam-Webster's,* which states that a soul is the ability of a person to feel kindness and sympathy to others. It is fair to say that a person with a soul can also feel the opposite emotions. This is the reason that I believe that a person's soul is influenced by different forces and powers – that is, light or darkness.

My experience with people of the dark side is that they are liars and manipulators, and they like to take what does not belong to them. They do this by means of witchcraft, and that's why God hates the practise of such dark forces: they get in the way of God's plan. From what I have also experienced and seen (and even read in the Bible), God uses the Devil to train His chosen soldiers. There are some secrets that God will reveal to His people, but only when we are the midst of action or on the battlefield.

Not only is the soul influenced by higher forces and power, but it is also owned by this divine force and power. For the most part, people haven't made a conscious decision in regards to who owns their souls. Therefore the soul falls within the parameters of default ownership, and this can be clearly seen by our actions and (to an extent) our interests.

Our souls affiliate with a divine or supernatural power, and we do not die but simply leave our physical bodies. However, as people we could still be fast asleep and not tuned into inner consciousness. Another way of putting it is that a person is not enlightened or not awakened. I also believe that if a person dies before she is awakened, her soul goes to default ownership. Again we are the secondary owners of our souls; the primary ownership of our souls is a conscious decision which we have to make. We are here for a reason, but we usually forget when we come to this time and space. I believe we knew it before we came, when we were in the spirit dimension.

My understanding is that we come for this experience to climb the ladder in the spirit world (the growing of our soul). The spirit world has ranks (Matt. 11:11 – 'the least in the kingdom of God is greater that John the Baptist'), and I think one of the ways for promotion in that realm is that we have to embark on a spiritual journey to planet earth. Depending what the mission is, it will determine all the logistics, such as the time of birth, the family of birth, and the country and location of birth. All these experiences are necessary to shape and mould us for our agreed assignment. We are certainly not alone here, because we all have invisible forces watching and guiding us. The more awake we are, the more insight we have about our mission. At that stage, we stop comparing our life experiences to others, and we start to comprehend our primary purpose on earth.

In many instances, we are gifted with the ability to perform and do many tasks very well, but it doesn't mean that is the mission we came here to fulfil. The only reason why it would or could be allowed for a season is to be able to learn from the experience and gain a skill that will help us in our mission.

The spirit world operates with accurate precision in terms of our mission, assignment, and timing of all activities. I know that there are still many unpleasant things that happen in our reality, but the reason we sense the unpleasantness is because we have emotions, and where we come from (spirit world), these emotions don't exist.

When we awaken, we give ownership of our soul over to the higher force, depending on our spiritual beliefs; that will be beginning of our journey. The mistake that some people make is that they relinquish the responsibility of their growth to other parties and people.

Enlightenment and awakening come in stages; the more it happens, the more we see the bigger picture. Our eyes really open – I mean our spiritual eyes – and we begin to see how shallow this world really is. Then we start to comprehend the state of consciousness the writers in our spiritual book experienced.

In regards to our awakening, it certainly has nothing to do with age. I have had conversations with a twenty-year-old and sensed spirituality and an awakening state of consciousness, and I have also have conversations with an eighty-year-old who didn't have any enlightenment. The eighty-year-old would obviously have more life experience than the twenty-year-old, but life experience and spirituality are two different things. This leads to what I would like to introduce next, which is soul evolution.

Personally, I believe some souls have lived before. What I mean is that they have lived in another life time and have reincarnated. Therefore, it is understandable that a twenty-year-could seem more enlightened than an eighty-year-old, because the twenty-year-old could possibly be an old or matured soul, whereas the eighty-year-old could be an infant or young soul.

This is best explained with music. A young singer might have an incredible singing voice and then hears the judges at the talent competition say things like, 'How old are you again? Where did the voice come from? How is that possible you're only ten?' In other worlds, that person could well as be an old soul, and that's the reason for the incredible ability without having had singing lessons. Also, the soul has a memory. There is so much that our souls and spirits know that our minds cannot comprehend.

The Development of the Human Soul

One could also use the word *progress* or *evolution* of the human soul. What this really means is reincarnation. In a religion like Christianity, such a term is hardly mentioned; however, there are many verses in the Bible that, if you read between the lines, show that's exactly what is being said.

For instance, when the disciples asked Jesus, 'Then why do the scribes say that Elijah must come first? He Replied, Elijah does come and will get everything stored and ready. But I tell that Elijah has come already, and they did not know or recognise him, but did to him as they like' (Matt. 17:10–12). Also in, Matthew 11:14 Jesus said, 'John himself is Elijah who was to come (before the kingdom).' It's also in Malachi 4:5.

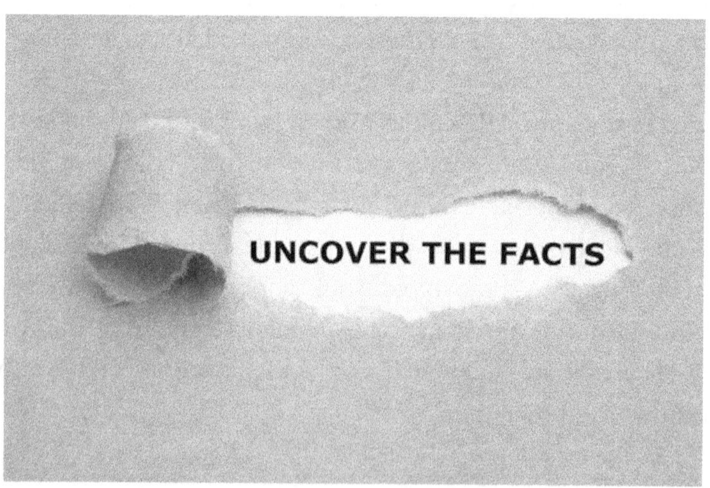

It's pretty obvious what the above verse means. To further prove this point, in the book of James, it states that Elijah was a man just like us (James 5:17). In other words, if John the Baptist was Elijah reincarnate, maybe we need to reconsider some of our thoughts. This will be discussed further in future chapters. Another verse comes to mind, and that is in Luke 9:18. Jesus asked His disciples, 'Who do people say that I

AM?' Their response was John the Baptist, Elijah, or an ancient prophet that has come back to life. Notice something very significant here: all the people His disciples mentioned were dead people. Jesus didn't rebuke them that their spiritual thinking was wrong; He simply said, 'Who do you say I AM.' It's fair to say in that time, it was a concept with which they were familiar.

To reiterate my stance, there is only one truth, and because a religion says nothing about a topic, that does not eliminate the truth of any particular concept. For the most part, this book will be from a Christian point of view. The reason is simply because Christianity is my faith. I try to use the word *religion* as little as possible; because it implies that I am following someone else's spiritual experience, whereas the whole point of spiritual books such as the Bible should be a guide. The Holy Spirit is the utmost teacher we will need, if you are of the Christian faith, and that's why we have verses like Jeremiah 33:3, which says, 'Call to Me and I will answer you and show you great and mighty things, fenced in and hidden, which you do not know (do not distinguish and recognize, have knowledge of and understand)' (Amplified Bible).

The fact that a person is of a particular faith does not mean that she is aware of the truth about certain topics. The above verse says great and mighty things, fenced in, and hidden. Simply put, there is a still load of significant information that has not been revealed to us.

I did come across some interesting literature on this topic of the human soul during my research, which I will share. Again, I reiterate that I sincerely believe there is one truth, and we humans may have various versions interpretations of it, but the fact still remains that one truth governs the human soul. Different religions and spiritual bodies may have part of this, but not necessarily the whole and full picture. Even from the perspective of my faith, Christianity, I still have many questions. The answers are not in the Bible and are not easily seen.

I came across this concept of the human soul, and it resonates with me. It's from the teachings of Michael, and it is a New Age teaching. I will leave to you to decide whether or not you believe in it. To summarise, it says that the human soul evolves and that there are thirty-five steps to complete the cycle. Also, each soul 'enters the physical plane as many times as is necessary to experience all aspects of life'. In doing so, the soul gradually evolves in consciousness, becoming more aware and self-aware, more capable and in control, more loving, less fearful, less isolated, and less unconscious (J. Steven, S. Warwick-Smith).

This is my take, and I base it on the lives of two great prophets. I also get the revelation from what has been written about these two prophets. Based on the Bible, I don't know how many times a soul comes back to time and space; however, I do believe that whatever we are called to do, we must qualify to do it. To qualify, we must have some life experience, and this I mean experience of the soul. According to the Bible, Elijah became the forerunner of Jesus. God also knew the soul of Jeremiah before he was in the womb. I believe we do keep on coming, but I don't know how many times.

Definition of Consciousness

I would best describe the word *consciousness* as the deep state of awareness of the spiritual element of what's in us and what's around us. It's part of the ability to discern what's not revealed by our five senses. Individuals can grow in levels of higher consciousness, and some people can choose to stay in a lower levels of consciousness. A lot of known spiritual people that we read about in our spiritual books knew the importance of developing the human consciousness. As a result of their actions, they reaped the benefits of being in that high state of mind. They grew into the know-how of how miracles were manifested. In order to get spiritual power, one has to understand that it comes with mastery; this requires transformation of one's consciousness to a higher place.

The obvious definition of consciousness is the state of mind of being conscious, but also the awareness of what's going on within and around us. When I say within, it's our thoughts, the feelings, and the sensations that we experience regularly about different situations. There is also a collective consciousness of groups of people; this differs from place to place. Different nations and cities have a different vibration about them.

A person would find an environment suitable if the vibration of the place resonates with them.

Consciousness and the soul are two concepts that go hand in hand, and they relate to our inner being. They are more meaningful to people of depth. Normally, people search for the meaning of why we are here and who we are as individuals. In order to answer the questions of who we are and our purpose, we must have awareness of who we are as individuals.

In the teachings of Michael, from the Michael handbook, it says that each of us is going through a long and often difficult process of reincarnating, living many different lives in many different circumstances. At the end of this learning process, when all there is for us to experience as a separable being has been experienced, our soul unites with others – about a thousand other souls who emerged into being at the same moment with us. This is our group of origin, known as an entity.

What is so fascinating with spiritual truth is that, if you don't seek, you don't find – and the more you seek, the more you find. A writer has the ability to set people free, because as people research, they find truth, and that gives them a better understanding to life. This leads to the question of what Jesus meant in Matthew 11:11.

An integrated entity is a far greater body of consciousness and intelligence than any single soul. Is that why Jesus said, 'Truly I tell you, among those born of women there has not risen anyone greater than John the Baptist: yet he who is least in the kingdom of heaven is greater than he' (Matt. 11:11)?

After reintegration, our souls are no longer separate fragments but are parts of a greater whole. I believe our individual souls are parts of something bigger in the spirit world.

Chapter 2

WHAT DIFFERENT RELIGIONS AND SPIRITUAL GROUPS SAY ABOUT THE HUMAN SOUL

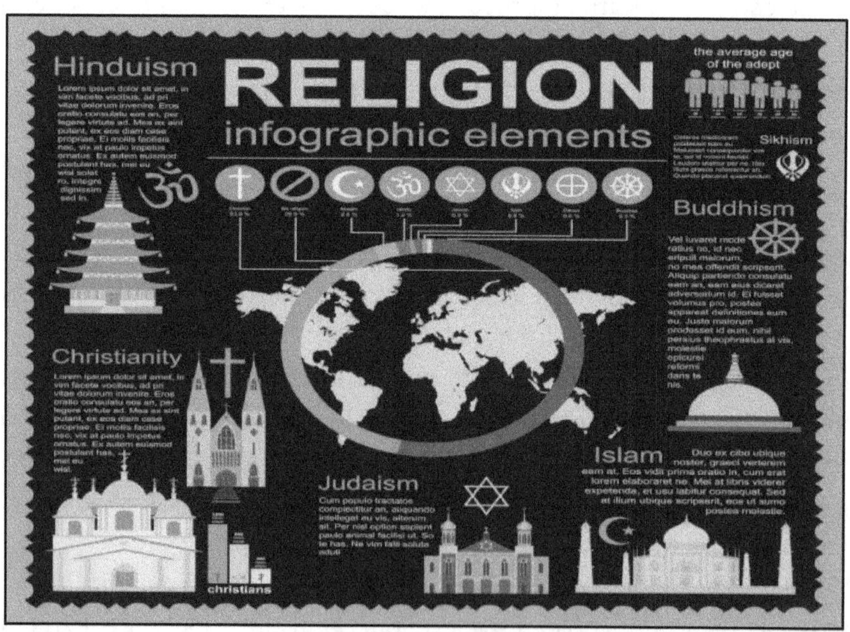

The common saying is we are spiritual beings having a human experience. It's a statement we take so lightly, but we need to ponder on it and have a full comprehension of what it actual means. Once we fully understand what it means, we then need to have a consistent, conscious awareness of not just its meaning but who we really are.

I put it this way: we are spirits in containers, and the containers happen to be our bodies. I have always known that most holy scriptures are coded, and it takes insight to understand what is really being said. The holy book that I am most familiar with is the Bible, so I will be making most of my references from it. However, I also believe a lot of good material was removed from

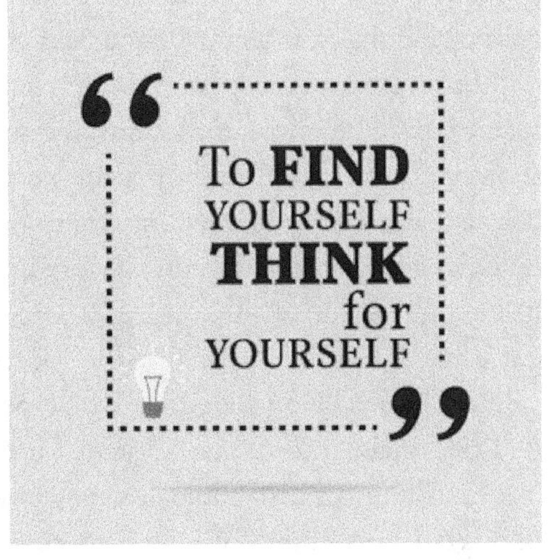

the Bible. Even different sect of Christianity have different books in their bible such as The Roman Catholic and the Protestant. Example would be, the book of Maccabees is in the Catholic bible but not in a Protestant bible.

As I always say, we need to read between the lines and ask for help from above (angels, Holy Spirit, etc.) for understanding. The main reason I say this is because of a verse in the Book of Genesis. This verse was from Jacob to Pharaoh, and I quote from Genesis 47: 9 'And Pharaoh asked Jacob, How old are you? Jacob said to Pharaoh, The days of the years of my pilgrimage are 130 years.'

What got my attention was the word *pilgrimage*. Let me give a little background about Jacob. His parents were Isaac and Rebekah, and Isaac was the son of Abraham. Jacob was the younger twin from Rebecca and Isaac; his brother was Esau and happened to be the older twin. Jacob was the spiritual one and walked with God, and it's pretty obvious when you walk with God, you have a deeper spiritual perception. Please don't take being religious and walking with God as the same thing. In my opinion, religion is man trying to control man and putting man in bondage.

Let's go back to the word *pilgrimage*. This word means 'to embark on a journey that has spiritual significance and value'. When I first saw the word in the verse, it dawned on me that he knew what was not perceived by a lot of people who walk the earth. It is also fair to say that Jacob's soul had grown, and that was why his name was changed to Israel.

I believe we all come here for several reasons, some primary and some secondary. The most important reason is the primary reason, which should not be confused with the secondary reason. In other words, because you can do something, that does mean it's what you should be doing at a certain point in time. More important, you have to follow your heart and be tuned into higher consciousness and the inner being to guide you. For Jacob to use the word randomly is what I mean by spiritual books being coded, and most people will overlook the word.

I personally believe that in order for us to grow in the spirit world (for our souls to grow), we come down to time and space for the experience to find wholeness above. We have to come down here and live, and that's why we are spirit beings undergoing a human experience: the reason is to grow our souls and find wholeness in consciousness.

When we can understand this, it will help us better understand our journey better and embrace it. No two lives are the same, and everybody's journey differs; this is what some religions don't explain, and some teachings of the gospel are, in my opinion, totally wrong.

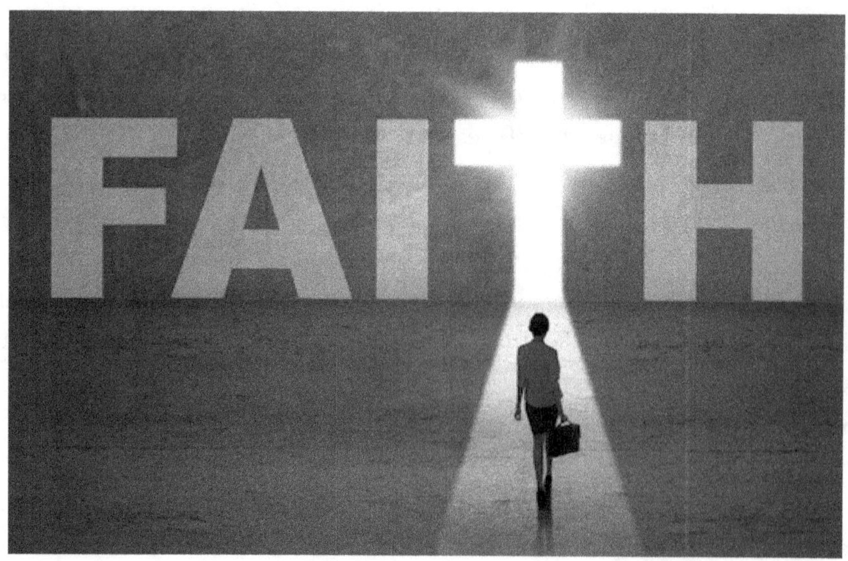

Another way to put it is that we are at different stages of learning, and we're here for different reasons. This has nothing to do with age, as has been mentioned earlier. As human beings, we all have desires, which is fine. For these desires to be manifested, they depend on some factors, such as appointed time, having faith to receive, and making sure nobody is using negative energy (black magic, witchcraft against you). The latter can be dealt with by having strong faith and getting your power from the light, which is God, via Jesus for Christians. This takes skill because the people of the dark side are wicked. Spiritual wisdom is needed in dealing with them. Once the Holy Spirit has revealed to you how to deal with them, diligence is required because your enemies are watching you night and day.

When a solid prayer life is established, then it has to be continuous; just like fitness, it's ongoing. We're still talking about faith here, and then the rest has to be left to the appointed time, which is in agreement to the reason why we came in the first place. Even the negative and painful situations in our lives could be part of the training for our task. Look at the life of Joseph, the son of Jacob. He was sold in to slavery, and some of his brothers wanted him dead. However, God was with him, and he was with God. The relationship with God is a two-way street. In James 4:8, God says, 'Draw near to Me and I will draw near to you.' As a matter of fact, we have to make the first move. I believe that Joseph knew this, and that's why God was always with Joseph: because Joseph was always with God. I will try not to go off the subject at hand and leave this for another book, but I think that's what we are missing in twenty-first-century Christianity.

As of 2016, the world's population stands at about 7.4 billion, out of which 2.3 billion (31.5 per cent) are of the Christian faith.

According to the Christian faith, to enter heaven, a soul has to believe in Jesus Christ as Lord. Also according to the faith, hell was created for the Devil and his fallen angels; these are also known as familiar spirits. Some human beings actually choose to possess these entities, so technically if this is still the case at point of death, they will go to the same place.

There are decent people in our world, and some are not religious or spiritual, but they are good people. My question is, where do their souls go?

In a later chapter, I will introduce the seven different spheres, and also the celestial sphere. The celestial sphere is also known as the kingdom of God, so that would be home to real Christians. I used the world *real* because not all people who claim to be Christians are true followers.

For the seven spheres that I just mentioned, entry into any of them is based on the condition of one's soul – I guess we term it as *judgement*. Also, let's look at this interesting verse from Jesus.

I assure you *and* most solemnly say to you, the person who hears My word [the one who heeds My message], and believes *and* trusts in Him who sent Me, has (possesses now) eternal life [that is, eternal life actually begins—the believer is transformed], and does not come into judgment *and* condemnation, but has passed [over] from death into life. (John 5:24, AMP)

This validates my point. The word *judgement* simply means the evaluation of evidence in order to make a decision. This evidence will come from the conditions of a person's soul. Everything we do in life is recorded, and this determines to what sphere a person goes. However I do believe that the other sphere will melt away, and only the celestial sphere will remain which will part of the new heaven.

If a person is a Christian, then the destination is the celestial sphere, which is the kingdom of God. The entry requirement is faith and belief in the Father and His Son Jesus, and not on the condition of one's soul.

However, I believe some Christians possess familiar spirits (practise dark magic) these people will not enter, Jesus would say I don't know you. I also have a feeling that anybody in spheres two through seven who wants to go to the celestial sphere has to come to time and space and be born again, because that's the only way to enter the kingdom of God, or maybe they can grow in the spirit world and graduate to the Kingdom of

God. From a biblical point of view the answer would be no (sphere one is hell).

I also believe that even from the celestial kingdom, some people come back on special assignment. However, many don't fulfil it because we get distracted trying to find the right path. That may be one of the reasons Jesus said many are called but few are chosen.

The next area I want to address is the soul development, which has been documented by Stevens et al. (1990). As we have seen from the Bible some souls do come back to live again (reincarnation). We have proved this in the case of Elijah being John the Baptist.

Let's look at this school of thought for a moment, and at the various soul stages.

There are five stages, and all of these stages have seven levels each. As mentioned above, the reason is to grow in consciousness. We described consciousness as 'the state of being conscious; awareness of one's existence, sensations, thoughts, surrounding'. We basically come to time and space to grow and develop our consciousness, which is ultimately our soul.

I personally believe that the spirit realm is perfect in every way, shape, and form. In order to grow and go higher in that dimension (there is a hierarchy in the spirit world), we have to come down to the physical world and get some training done, so to speak. There is also an element of growth and learning that takes place in the spirit world.

Here are the five stages.

1. Infant Soul
2. Baby Soul
3. Young Soul
4. Mature Soul
5. Old Soul

Stage	Focus	Learning Experiences
Infant souls	Being alive	Survival, physicality, mortality, environmental awareness
Baby souls	Belonging to a culture	Rules, roles, law and order, social awareness
Young souls	Being a free agent	Independence, self- advancement, personal achievement, free will
Matured souls	Coexistence with others	Interdependence, relationships, empathy, intimacy, self-awareness
Old souls	Being part of all that is	Autonomy, non-attachment, wise counsel, spiritual awareness

I am not going to go into the levels – for a detailed study **check out** *The Michael Handbook* **published by Warwick Press**. What I find fascinating is the stages, and I must say they resonate with my consciousness, to the extent that sometimes when I interact or engage with a person, the person's attitude to life, conversation, and mannerisms seldom give me an indication of what type of soul that person is. Personally, I like to believe that I am an old soul, but it's something a person grows to comprehend by taking account of one's journey in life, and by knowing that the painfulness of the ride is for a reason. My experiences have shaped me, and I learnt a lot from them.

I believe the journey is to help us come into oneness with God, as well as to help other people along their spiritual journeys.

Along with this school of thought, they (the new age movement) obviously believe that people live various lives, which depends on their stage and level. As we mentioned with Elijah being John the Baptist, the verse that also comes to mind is Jeremiah 1:5. 'Before I formed you in the womb I knew [and] approved of you [as my chosen instrument], and before you were born I separated and set you apart, consecrating you; [and] I appointed you as a prophet to the nations' (Amplified Bible).

Let's break this verse down, and what I feel in my spirit to be true. The first line of the verse says before we were in a mother's womb. This means before we were conceived, we existed. Some souls dwell in the spirit world, and for God to approve of Jeremiah, Jeremiah's soul was in heaven and must have had a high degree of spiritual magnitude. The reason I say this is because to be called to be a prophet requires high qualities of character, which I would say is an old soul, that's why God said I knew you.

Even if a person is a matured or old soul, they grow into it, here in time and space. Also, going back to the verse, God said, 'I knew you and approved of you.' What did God know and approve of? It can only be one thing, and that is Jeremiah's soul. The fact is that we are made of body, mind, soul, and spirit. Both body and mind had not been formed then, but the verse says, 'before I formed you'. This verse alone quantifies all I have mentioned about the human soul so far.

Evolution of the soul comes about by experiencing life in many different ways, making important choices within those life experiences, and learning from the consequences of those choices. Key experiences and choices are set up by the soul in spirit before each lifetime (see the concept of life plan, **discussed later).** Some believe that one life is not enough to experience the full spectrum of life circumstances and choices. That makes sense, because what I am leaning in this life has taken so long to grasp. The important question we should ask ourselves is, Why do some people know more about the mysteries of life than others? Better still, why are some people more interested about the mysteries than others. Why are some people nice and sweet, and some are pure evil? The answers to these questions lie within **parameters of** the age of a person's soul and who owns the soul.

A matured or old soul can easily understand deep spiritual truth without trying too hard, and this is because our souls have a memory. This enables them to understand what really matters, and they see the bigger picture with the eye of the spirit. An old soul wonders why some people act silly, evil, and heartless, but quickly understands that it has to do with the age of the person's soul.

Some people are old souls but are unaware of the fact. In a situation like this, life has to create situations that will isolate the individual, so that the person can go deep within. A person who doesn't fit in, can be a clue that the old soul is here on a mission but needs isolation to find, hear, identify, and know the voice of God. We see this pattern in the life of Moses and the apostle Paul. A good example from our time is Nelson Mandela, who had to be isolated for twenty-six years to find himself and fulfil his mission.

Life Plan

There is a detailed life plan for each individual soul, which includes the life events that are to take place. This plan would be systematically put together by God or some might say our spirit guide, while the soul in question is still in the spirit. From study and understanding of scripture, this plan is not automatic; as the Bible says, many are called but few are chosen. I believe we agree to the plan in the spirit world, but a person can drift once one is in the time and space reality. God does give us free will, and He will do everything to get our attention. However we have to want it also. If a person senses that there is a calling on his/ her life, and then he has to stay close to God, it is also called walking with God. The reason is that the closer a person is to God, the easier it is to hear God's voice and be directed by Him. I am certainly not talking about religions, because they could be a person's greatest enemy; most of them will manipulate individuals and steal the gift of what God has really called am person to do. Always be careful of those close to you – family, so-called friends, and others. You must live in higher consciousness, on a higher plane, if God's plan for your life is different from the ordinary. A Christian will call it living in the spirit, and it's also the same as walking with God. This way God will show the plans of your enemies and communicate the necessary steps and action to take. Bear in mind that people try to steal others' spiritual gifts. That's why it's important to stay close to God. I will write about this in another book.

The life plan constitutes the necessary experiences that the soul has to undertake in order for the purpose to be accomplished; obviously, this would include pleasant and unpleasant situations. Also in the plan will be other souls to be involved at different time frames. There will be no recollection of any such plan when the soul in question gets

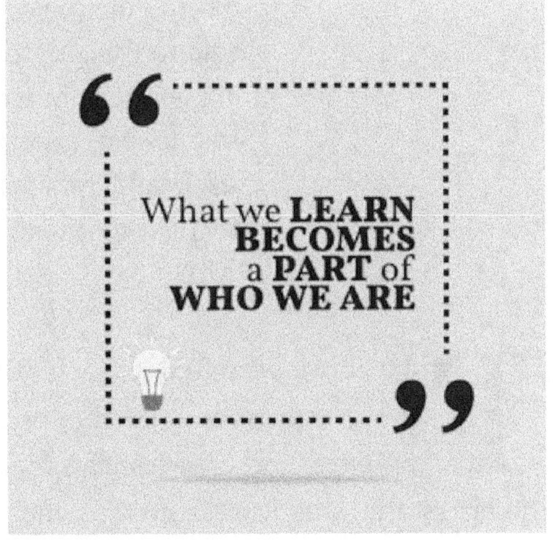

to the time and place (temporary amnesia). This will enable the plan to be experienced in totality with all necessary steps along the way. I have mentioned something similar when I looked at the belief of the Judaism sect Kabbalah, as well as Islam.

Chapter 3

THE MANY DWELLING PLACES (SPHERES)

In My Father's house are many dwelling places. If it were not so, I would have told you, because I am going there to prepare a place for you. And if I go and prepare a place for you, I will come back again and I will take you to Myself, so that where I am you may be also. And [to the place] where I am going, you know the way.' Thomas said to Him, 'Lord, we do not know where You are going; so how can we know the way?' Jesus said to him, '[a]I am the [only]Way [to God] and the [real] Truth and the [real] Life; no one comes to the Father but through Me. (John 14:2-7, AMP)

The above verse unlocks a lot of the mystery of the spirit world. As I mentioned in the previous chapter, we have seven spheres and a celestial sphere. The celestial sphere is also known as the kingdom. Entry to the seven spheres is based on the condition of one's soul, but the celestial sphere is the highest, and entry is based on faith in Jesus.

I like to believe that Jesus was referring to the spheres when He said 'in my Father's house there are many dwelling places (mansions)'. As already mentioned, faith in Jesus is the entry requirement, and it's fair to say that's what Jesus meant when He replied to Thomas and said, 'I Am the only way to God (the Celestial Sphere).'

The other spheres will be based on the condition of a person's soul, and I see this in John 5:24.

I assure you and most solemnly say to you, the person who hears My word [the one who heeds My message], and believes and trusts in Him who sent Me, has (possesses now) eternal life [that is, eternal life actually begins—the believer is transformed], and does not come into judgment and condemnation, but has passed [over] from death into life.

When we talk about spiritual matters, it's is based on insight and revelation. Some people catch the revelation quicker than others. It's important that we know that things of the spirit are not science; more often than not we can't prove them, but it's an inner knowing with strong conviction. Sometimes the human mind can't comprehend it, but the feeling is so strong in one's spirit. In fact, it is through our spirits that God speaks to us.

Go back to John 5:24. Jesus said that those who believe and trust in Him have eternal life and do not come into judgement. It's important that we understand what the word actually means. Most people think that the meaning implies an outcome, but that is wrong. As I said earlier, it is basically an evaluation of evidence in order to make a decision. Therefore the outcome of a judgement could also be positive. Comparing it to a natural court of law, the judge and members of the jury are always evaluating evidence so they can reach a decision, which is ultimately the judgement.

As previously indicated, we have a world population of about seven billion, and 30 per cent of are Christians. I believe the kingdom (celestial sphere) is the best dwelling place, and I believe the other dwelling places could be the spheres.

On arrival at the spirit world, a soul's mental, moral, and spiritual condition will indicate the initial place of such soul. Spheres are spiritual dwellings where the human soul goes after leaving the physical plane. Spheres have different degrees of light; there is also a sphere of darkness. For instances from spheres two to seven (seven is the highest), the light brightens in progression to the hierarchy of the levels. The celestial sphere is also called the kingdom, heaven, or even paradise; all these descriptive words are talking about the same place. Basically, it is where God dwells, and it has the highest form of light amongst all the spheres.

The sphere we go to is dependent on the condition of our souls at the time we die. Everything we have ever done is recorded, and our souls have a memory of all our deeds. The vibration of our souls will ultimately take us to the sphere that matches the condition of our souls.

According to Culter (2011), when a soul leaves the body, its first destination is the buffer zone, a neutral place between the earth plane and the first sphere. I believe this is the first part of the tunnel that people with near-death experience explain, and it is grey in colour. Some people say it's this place that departed souls make contact with loved ones in the earth realm. They may stay for a short period, maybe until their burial has taken place. Then they go through the tunnel.

Picture 7. Spheres & the celestial sphere.

My experience from this, having lost both of my parents, is that there is a sense of the departed presence around a person. This could be a feeling that you know the person who just passed away is nearby; it could also be by confirmed in a dream.

First Sphere (Black Layer)

This is the nearest sphere to the earth, and it has the least light or no light. It is what we call hell, the home of bad spirits (demons). People also go here depending on the condition and contents their souls. I believe if a person possesses an unclean spirit at time of death, or has transacted his soul, he could end up here.

Second Sphere

This is referred to as the sphere of familiarity, and the reason is simple. It basically looks like the earth – not identical but similar in the infrastructure, and with recognition of people they once knew. This where ordinary people go to if they lived in the best way possible but were not spiritual in nature. In this sphere, souls learn to use their spiritual powers with help from more advanced spirits. This power is used to get everything they need, such as houses and clothes.

Cutler (2011) also says that souls in these spheres may have a season of confusion, such as having the anticipation that they were going to be in the presence of God and Jesus, when that's not the case. They have found their destination in a lower place. When they do receive visitations from Jesus, they do not recognise Him, and Jesus cannot really display Himself as He is, because His spiritual brightness is far too powerful for this lower sphere; He can't really make Himself known.

Third Sphere

This sphere is called the first heavenly realm in the spirit world. It's mainly occupied by people who were devoted to their path while on earth or since being in the spirit world. The souls here have also developed the quality of their love. The place is beautiful with very nice facilities.

The level of love and spiritual knowledge is high in this sphere, and souls use their advance nature to help others develop. This is also a sphere where they can perceive the will of God.

Fourth Sphere

This is an intellectual sphere. There are different paths souls could chose to follow. Some follow the intellectual and natural love path, whereas some follow the divine love path. In this sphere, souls are not really interested in the affairs of the world but still care for people of the world. The divine love path spends almost no time here.

Fifth Sphere

This is considered the soul sphere, and people following the intellectual and natural love path spend no time here. This sphere is necessary and important for those following the divine love path.

Sixth Sphere

This is the highest sphere for those who follow the intellectual and the natural love path to their spiritual development. This is the peak of the intellectual path. Perfect natural man reaches mental limits. Souls do not progress beyond the sixth sphere without divine love. It is believed that this sphere is not in possession of absolute truth. Souls in this sphere do go beyond this sphere. The question is what happens to these souls when the new heavens and a new earth is established. The old souls will pass away. This prophesy is seen throughout the Bible, from the Old Testament right to the last book of the New Testament, in Isaiah 65:17, Isaiah 66:22, 2 Peter 3:13, and finally Revelation 21:1. What is also interesting is that heaven in these verses is plural. Unless a soul in this sphere aspires for divine love, it could pass away with the current earth and current heaven.

Seventh Sphere

This is the highest sphere for people who have chosen the divine love of the Father. All the spiritual knowledge that needs to be known has come to them, and they are in transition to go to the celestial heavens (the kingdom of God). Souls in this sphere have immortality. The route to the seventh sphere is through the third and then the fifth.

Celestial Kingdom

Souls reborn through love become like divine angels. Matthew 22:30 states, 'For in the resurrection they neither marry nor are given in marriage, but are like angels in heaven.'

Only souls transformed by the new birth are eligible to enter the divine kingdom of God (born again). I think it's fair to say that souls in spheres two, four, and six can only enter the celestial sphere by coming down to time and space. I also wonder why God draws some souls to Jesus but not others. Jesus says in John 10:29, 'My Father, who has given them to Me, is greater than all; and no one is able to snatch them out of My Father's hand.' I can't help but ponder on this verse. The question is, why would God give some souls to Jesus and not all souls? With God, we know He gives allowance for our free will. God will never force anything on us. Could it be that these souls desired to have divine love, and this could only come by having a relationship with Jesus? This supports my thinking that in order for people in the sixth sphere to go higher into the celestial sphere, they must first come to time and place. God points and gives these souls to Jesus. Otherwise, why would God give some souls and not all to Jesus? It's something to think about.

The new heavens mentioned in the Bible will only be the spiritual kingdom of God, and the other spheres (heavens) will pass away.

The Spiritual Kingdom

This is also known as the celestial sphere, where souls have been redeemed by divine love and mercy of God. This is the place for those souls who believed in Jesus as the Son of God and accepted Him as Lord and Saviour.

This new realm is above the seventh sphere, and according to spiritualism and beyond, it is a new realm known as the kingdom. They stated that it's not as ancient as the seven spheres, because it is just over two thousand years old. This coincides with the death of Jesus Christ.

This kingdom is actually independent of the state of the soul. I guess this sums up the salvation message, by having faith in Jesus Christ.

However, as mentioned earlier, the requirements of this celestial sphere are independent of the condition of the soul. Not everybody who professes to be redeemed by divine love is redeemed, as Jesus said in Matthew 7:23 in the Weymouth New Testament. 'And then I will tell them plainly, "I never knew you: be gone from me, you doers of wickedness."' I believe the reason for Jesus's reply to this is that some churches combine other powers which are not from God, ie witchcraft, and use the power of familiar spirits.

Ultimately, in the celestial sphere, those redeemed by divine love and the mercy of God possess the gift of immortality. They have souls so well developed that they are part of God's divine nature. Finally, universal spirituality states that our souls continue to grow in the divine love and perfection until we get in the presence of the Father and are able to see Him with increasingly clear soul perceptions.

Chapter 4

THE ABRAHAMIC RELIGIONS' VIEW ON THE AFTERLIFE

The three main Abrahamic religions are Islam, Judaism, and Christianity. They are called the Abrahamic religions because they share the patriarch Abraham in their lineage. Having said that, his role differs in the three religions. Christianity and Judaism are very similar, if not the same, in regards to the Old Testament.

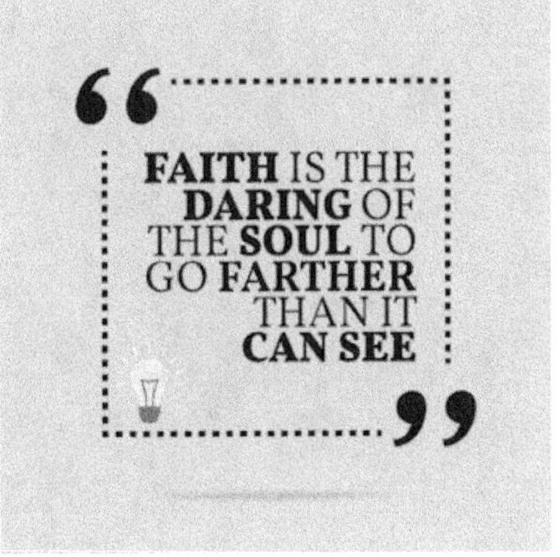

The picture shows Prophet Elijah raises the son of the widow of Zarephath from the dead.

1. Judaism

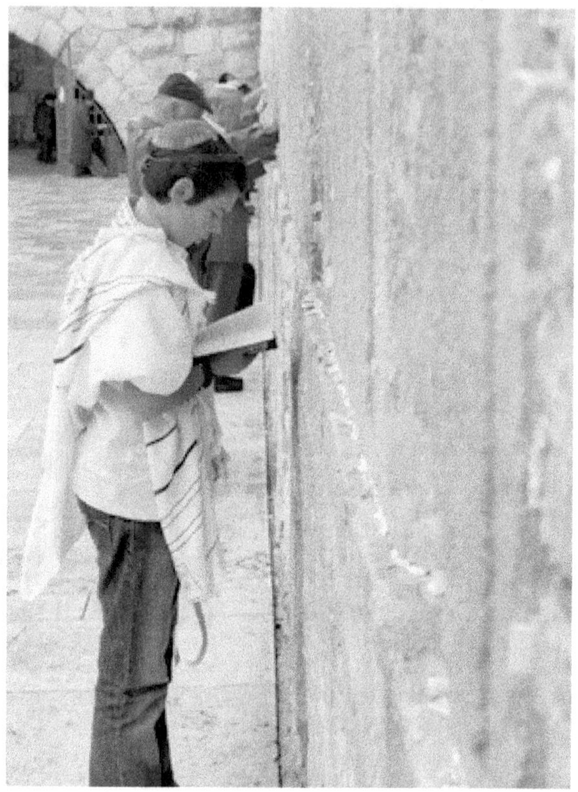

Judaism is the foundational faith that led to both Christianity and Islam. Actually, the Torah is what is known as the Old Testament in the Christian Bible. Also, the Quran has references to both the Old and New Testaments, but some of the stories differ in concept.

In Judaism, it is believed that nothing happens to the soul when we die, and that the souls will be resurrected when God decides it's time. Death in this religion does mean separation of soul and body, and the soul goes to the spirit world. The Book of Daniel, which is part of the Torah, states in verse 12:2, 'And many of them that sleep in the dust of the earth shall awake, some to everlasting life, and some to shame and everlasting contempt.' Basically, they believe the soul is going to sleep until Judgement Day.

o   Young boy and other people praying in front of the Wailing Wall, Jerusalem, Israel.

However, Kabbalah, which originated from Judaism, is known as an esoteric and mystical school of thought. It has a different perspective on the human soul when we die. The Kabbalah believes in the migration of the human soul and reincarnation. They believe we have two distinct souls.

They call the first soul Nefesh HaBehamit, and this is the soul they believe brings the body to life. This soul inhabits powers such as pleasure, will, intellect, and emotions. Some say Nefesh HaBehamit wishes to fulfil the base needs, passion, and desires of the body. They refer to it as self- centred part of the soul. Also from this part of the soul, we have negative character traits such as anger, apathy, and arrogance. It's similar to what a Christian calls the flesh.

The second soul is called Nefesh Elokit. This soul is believed to be described by Job as a 'Part of God', and it existed before it came into the body and will exist when it leaves the body. It is also known as the divine soul, and it's the source of good inclinations and godly desires. Again, it's similar to what a born-again Christian calls living in the spirit.

Prior to coming to this time and place, Nefesh Elokit is taken on a heavenly tour. It is shown all the aspects of the Garden of Eden, and it is also shown hell (Gehinom). The soul is made aware of the implications of the journey (which is perilous in nature, potentially dangerous, and risky), as well as the distractions and enticements that will be encountered. The soul is then made to make a declaration of promise that it will be faithful and true, will maintain a right standing with God, and will stay humble during the journey. The soul is then given all the spiritual strength and nourishment required to change Nefesh HaBehamita and its part in the world.

This part of the soul, Nefesh Elokit, is part of God. Therefore its attention is set towards divinity. It has a structure in place for pleasure, will, intellect, and emotions. Again, all these are to gratify divinity rather than on oneself.

Therefore when a soul comes to earth, it is comprised of both Nefesh Elokit and Nefesh HaBehamit, and they both function in the thinking mind. They live together for the duration of the journey, both trying to gain control of the thinking mind. (This school of thought is very similar to what born-again Christians will call the flesh and the spirit).

Upon death, Nefesh Elokit will return to the spirit world, and the soul will be judged based on the activities during its pilgrimage. It is also believed that for every Mizvah (good deeds) a person embarked upon, the person will receive a defending angel, and every misdeed done in a person's life will represent an accusing angel. Basically, a person will be judged based on the condition of one's soul, which has recorded everything we do in our lifetime. It's fair to say that all spiritual bodies and religions agree and believe this.

To reiterate, the Jewish tradition believes the human soul has three parts: Nefesh, Ruach, and Neshama. The Bible also says in Hebrews 4:12 that the word of God is full of power and sharp, because it penetrates the dividing lines of the soul. We can also change the word *dividing* to *divisions*, which basically means the soul has different parts and levels.

Nefesh can be described as the lowest part of the soul. It's what the Christian will call fleshly, and it's all about human desire. The second part is Ruach; this part of the soul can distinguish between good and evil, and hence it's called the middle section of the soul. Finally, we have the Neshama. This is the highest part of the soul, also known as the godly part, which can be developed to go to higher levels of consciousness. As a result, a person can receive spiritual elevation and be God-minded. This part of the soul lives after death.

According to the *Jewish Encyclopaedia*, the Jewish belief is that all souls are prepared before the foundation of the world. The human mind can't comprehend this, but the human spirit can. The spiritual knowledge revealed to our senses is limited in this dimension; however, people can be elevated in consciousness and gain insight into the mysteries of our world from the spirit world. We are dual spirit beings that have the potential to be in two dimensions – that is, in the spirit dimension and in this time and space dimension. This is also along the same lines as the teaching of the apostle Paul: God called His followers before the foundation of the earth. Such insight is given to a person from the spirit dimension, and it can only be understood by being in an elevated state of mind.

Part of Paul's writing is that the righteous who come into the world are preordained from the beginning. All souls are therefore pre-existent, although the number of those that are to become incorporated is not determined at the very start. As a matter of fact, there are souls of different quality. Solomon says, 'Now I was a child of parts, and a good soul fell to my lot; nay, rather, being good, I came into a body undefiled.' The body returns to earth when its possessor 'is required to render back the soul which was lent him'.

It is also believed by some that the soul is attached to a baby after twenty-two weeks of conception, and that the first time the baby kicks in the mother's womb is a sign that the soul is attached. Such a concept may be hard to prove by logic, but things of the spirit can't be comprehended with logic – it's by enlightenment.

From the above text, it is mentioned that the souls existed in the spirit world. In fact, it goes on to say before the foundation of the world. This is in line with Paul's teaching in Ephesians 1:4 'We were chosen in Him before the foundation of the world.' This means we existed in the spirit world before the world was created; we existed as souls. In Paul's verse above, it says we were chosen beforehand. This also reminds me of

Jeremiah 1:5. 'When God said before the prophet was formed in his mother's womb, He [God] said I knew and approved of you.' Again, this is soul form. Based on both these verses, in order to be chosen and approved of, some form of merit was recognised in these souls.

My question is, how do we gain merit in the spirit world? The answer I can think of is that the soul must first come to time and space like Jacob and go on a pilgrimage. When scriptures talk about the time before the foundation of the world, isn't it fair to say that it is the foundation of my world, which would be before I was born? My foundation started when I came out of the womb, but my soul existed long before that. I also believe that souls can also learn and grow in the spirit world.

2. Islam

This religion has a lot of references to the Torah and the Old Testament because it has its origins from Hagar and Ishmael. Abraham fathered Ishmael, Hagar's son.

Picture of the wailing wall and Al Aqsa Mosque in Jerusalem, Israel.

In this religion, death is merely a movement from one world to another. Some in this religion believe that we start our journey from our mothers' wombs. That is, 120 days after conception, the soul is blown into the foetus. In Ahmed's review article (2008), the soul journeys to the mother's womb four months after conception, the soul is then blown into the fetus.

A human being is put in a mothers womb in forty days and becomes a clot of thick blood for a similar period, then a piece of flesh for a similar period. Then Allah sends an angel, who is ordered to write four things. He is ordered to write down the new creature's deeds, his livelihood, his date of death, and whether he will be blessed or wretched (in religion). Then the soul is breathed into him.

This is in line with other spiritual beliefs that I have come across. Our lives are shown to us before we come, including what we are supposed to do. That's why we need to be in tune with the Holy Spirit, so we can be led by the Lord. When we are determined to do what we are really destined to do, we should be ready for opposition. That's why Jesus had to tell off Peter, His disciple. 'But Jesus turned and said to Peter, "Get behind Me, Satan! You are a stumbling block to Me; for you are not setting your mind on things of God, but on things of man."'

Only our heart can understand what God wants you to do, and there is no way in the world you can do it without the Holy Spirit. Even still, agents of Satan will be all around to distract and to try to point us in another direction. The truth is that these agents of the Devil are so diligent in what they do that we have to cling to Jesus Christ. As they song goes, 'I need you, Lord, I need you.' The song says every hour, but I think we need the Lord's help every second.

Islam believes we have no say or choice about who our parents would be, as well as our race, colour, and nationality. Allah is aware of this before our birth as we continue our journey to fulfil our destiny. As a person of the Christian faith, I also believe the family, country, and culture we come from is dependent on what our mission is, because the passage we go through is meant to train us and equip us for the journey. As our eyes start to open spiritually, we will begin to understand that no part of our journey was a mistake. Even when we miss the mark, the Lord and His helpers will work to get us back on track.

Doing the Lord's will is certainly not a walk in the park, and that why we have those stories in the Bible: not only to encourage us, but also to state what we have to overcome in order to fulfil our purpose and mission.

Some in Islam believe that in our lifetime, the soul and body are together except during sleep. The soul may leave the body and come back in the morning. This goes back to my principle that there is only one truth. Some religions may be on track, and some may not be, but God will point out who was in truth and who was in error. Our job is to love our neighbours as ourselves, and to not judge.

This religion also believes no one knows how, when, and where one will die; it's up to the creator. I do know God can reveal things about our lives to us, even the time of our promotion to the spirit world. The other thought that comes to mind is that there are certainly times when the kingdom of darkness takes out people, because we know their kingdom is wicked and it's simply their nature to act in such ways.

 Young Muslim girl reading the Quran.

The only way stop the wicked kingdom of darkness from prevailing is to be strong in spirit.

They also say no one has the right to take his own life; if the person does, he should automatically go to hell. I personally don't agree that the soul will go to hell; however, the person did not pass the test of life, and this will affect the person's place in spirit world. The giver of life is the only one who has the right to take life.

If we knew the implications of our actions in this time and space, I can assure you that so many things would be done different. From my observation, it seems like the young, baby, and infant souls often act carelessly, especially in regards to hurting other souls. Matured or old souls will always know better, especially when they have come to the full realisation of who they are.

In Islam, they believe that when a person's time is up, the angel of death comes to take the soul and puts it in a place called Barzakh; then it is brought back to the Lord.

The word *Barzakh* is Arabic and means separation or barrier. It's the barrier between the physical and the spiritual worlds, in which the souls awaits after death and before resurrection on Judgement Day. (All Abrahamic religions believe there will be a Day of Judgement.)

It is also believed that for a person who led a life of evil, the removal of the soul is tough and difficult. In such situations, more than one angel has to work together to beat the back and face of the deceased in order to remove the soul.

However if a person lived a good life, the soul comes out with ease because it yearns to meet the Lord. This resonates with me because the people who are afraid of death are fearful for a reason. All I can say is change your ways before it's too late. For instance, in the case of a person who lived a good life, a light like the sun and a sweet fragrance comes out to the soul.

Muslims believe that for souls about to leave this world and move to the next world, angels with faces as bright as the sun descend from heaven, and they sit around the deceased soul in throngs as far as the eye can see. The angel of death then sits at the head of the deceased soul and says, 'Good soul come out to forgiveness and receive pleasure from Allah.'

The soul is then taken through a company of angels, and they ask, 'Who is this good soul?' The answer is 'So-and-so, the son of so- and-so,' using the best names that the deceased soul was called in the world. The soul is then bought to the lowest heaven, and the angels ask the gates to open for the soul. When the gates are opened for the soul, then angels who are near Allah from each of the heavens accompany the soul to subsequent heavens, until the soul reaches the heaven where Allah dwells.

The soul is registered in the book and then returns to its body. Two angels come to the soul, tell the soul to sit up, and ask the soul, 'Who is your Lord, and what your religion?' If the soul replies that his Lord is Allah and his religion is Islam, a voice from on high declares the truth has been spoken. Out spreads carpets from the garden from for the soul, and the gates of the garden open for the soul.

They believe the opposite is the case for an unbeliever. It goes through the same process and is referred to as a foul soul. The soul of the unbeliever is taken to the lowest heaven, and when the gates are asked to be opened, they do not open. The gates of heaven are not open, and neither will the soul enter the garden. The soul is then registered in his book of the lowest earth.

When the soul returns to its body and then two angels come and ask, 'Who is your Lord?' if the soul says it doesn't know, a voice will come from high and say, 'Spread out carpets from fire for the soul, and open a gate of the fire.'

What I want to point out here is that before gate of the garden and heaven could open, the soul had to indicate who its Lord was. I find a lot of similarity in the Christian faith in this regards, because it is written, 'Believe in the Lord Jesus Christ, and you shall be saved.'

In this religion, they postulate about rebirth and judgement. However, the important aspect of it all is that before these two could take place, the gate of the garden and heaven must of being opened first. The same applies to Christianity: simply because we believe in Jesus Christ as Lord, that does not exempt us from judgement.

But the judgement will be different from a person who never had faith in Jesus before his death. The Bible also says in 1 Peter 4:17 that judgement will begin in God's household first. We must remember that judgement simply means gathering of evidence to make a decision.

In regards to rebirth, for specific missions, it has to be based on the merit of that particular soul, which is developed by having pilgrimage experiences and also growing in the spirit world. What we do know is that there are ranks in the spirit world, as Jesus said in regarding John the Baptist, 'Saying in the Kingdom of Heaven, John is the least.' My own understanding of this verse is that there is obviously a hierarchy in the kingdom (and John is in the least of them), and that we are not individuals in the spirit world and are of a group of one. For instance, a group of a thousand souls together may represent one entity or person.

All I can say is that we will never fully comprehend the spirit world and the afterlife. The Bible even says that we know in part and we prophesy in part (1 Cor. 13:9). Having said that, I also place confidence in Jeremiah 33:3, in which God asks us to call upon Him and ask, and He would tell us great and mysterious things.

3. Christianity

Technically, the Christian faith does not believe in reincarnation; however, there are scriptures that could indicate otherwise. I do understand the concept that reincarnation and salvation don't agree. I also do believe in the finished works of Jesus and the cross. One thing can be certain: we only know part of the truth and mysteries of life, death, and our souls. As I already mentioned, the Bible also says, 'for we know in part, and we prophesy in part ... for we see through a glass, darkly.'

Personally, as a Christian I believe in the finished works of the cross, and I also believe that some people do come back. But it's not about what I believe. Let's analyze the scriptures we have, because who knows whether some verses were removed from the original text?

 The Rapture of people out of this world.

Let's start with Elijah, because we know he reincarnated as John the Baptist. This was first prophesied by the prophet Malachi and was later confirmed by Jesus Himself. See the following verses.

Behold I will send you Elijah the prophet before the coming of the great and dreadful day of the LORD. (Mal. 4:5)

And if you are willing to receive it and accept it John himself is Elijah who was to come before the Kingdom…. Jesus says He who has ears to hear, let him be listening and let him consider and perceive and comprehend by hearing. (Matt. 11:14–15, AMP)

 Picture of John the Baptist, baptizing Jesus. John was the forerunner of Jesus. Reincarnate Elijah

This alone is enough for me to believe that some people do come back. I personally believe a lot of great spiritual figures in the Bible's days did come back then, and do come back now. I believe depending on your agreed task in time and space, certain lifetime experiences are required. Actually, sometimes I can tell by the wisdom and insight that comes from a person's mouth; obviously I will take age into consideration.

What I believe Jesus is saying in verse 15 is that he was cautioning us with words such as *consider, perceive,* and *comprehend by hearing.* Basically, He was saying we should carefully think about it, reflect on it, and examine what He said in verse 14 (John the Baptist is Elijah). Finally, He told us to be aware of the fact that John the Baptist is Elijah.

If it happened, then it is still happening now because God does not change. He is the same yesterday, today, and forever, and because God does not change, neither does His mode of operation change.

Jeremiah and Elijah were both prophets, and I believe that such people have to be old souls, people who have been here before.

 Elijah taken to heaven by a whirlwind.

The second scripture I would like to use to open us up to the possibility that maybe the early church knew what we don't in regards to reincarnation is John 9:2. 'And the disciples asked him, saying Master, who did sin, this man, or his parents, that he was born blind?'

The first part of the question implies to a previous life. The fact that they asked the question – and that Jesus didn't say the question was wrong spiritually or that they have missed how the kingdom of heaven operated as we know He did in teaching His disciples – should make us question the possibility of the subject at hand.

Another important verse that got me thinking is Jeremiah 1:5, in which God told Jeremiah that before he was formed in his mother's womb, God knew Jeremiah and approved of him.

Some questions come to mind about this verse, such as 'before I formed you'. To me, that means before Jeremiah's body was formed, God knew him and approved of him. We know it wasn't his body, and it wasn't spirit because we are created in the image of God, and God's spirit is put in us, especially in the case of a prophet. What we have left is the human soul.

The human soul exists independent of the body, and it existed before the body. That's what God knew and approved of. The question is how we gain ranks or increase in levels in the spirit world.

A person has to go on a pilgrimage, which is basically a journey, a physical experience in the physical world. When Pharaoh asked Jacob's age, he answered by saying, 'The years of my pilgrimage is so-and-so.' Another important point is that we can be called in the spirit world to come down to the physical world for an assignment, but we have to qualify to be chosen when we get here in time and space.

The Bible goes on to say that we are destined to live only once – see Hebrews 9:27–28.

Just as man is destined to die once, and after that to face judgment, so Christ was sacrificed once to take away the sins of many people; and he will appear a second time, not to bear sin, but to bring salvation to those who are waiting for him.

As we can see in the verses, we only live once. As much as I believe that the book of Hebrews is a great book, I can't help but ask who wrote it. Was the name of the writer omitted due to error, or intentionally? If by error, then how many more errors do we have in the Bible? Was the writer's name was intentionally omitted, and why?

Finally, with these verses, we have to read between the lines. Let's start with Luke 9:20. Jesus asked His disciples, 'But whom do the people say the people say that I am?' The following answers were given to Jesus: John the Baptist, Elijah, and one of the ancient prophets come back to life. Their answers were not correct, but all their answers were people who had lived before. That tells me the disciples and people of the time were familiar with people reincarnating. At the time Jesus asked the question, John the Baptist had been killed by Herod. Jesus didn't rebuke them and say they were spiritually incorrect; if they had been, Jesus would have said so. All Jesus said was, 'Who do you say I am?'

The last passage I want you to consider is John 9:1–3. Again, Jesus did not rebuke them for them being spiritual in correct. Here are the verses, and as Jesus passed by, he saw a man which was blind from His birth.

And his disciples asked him, saying, Master, who did sin, this man, or his parents, that he was born blind?

Jesus answered, neither hath this man sinned, nor his parents: but that the works of God should be made manifest in him.

Basically, they asked if the blind man had sinned; he was born blind, and obviously implies the blind man had sinned in his previous life.

I think some of Jesus's teachings were omitted from the Bible. (I sense something missing in some places. For example, the Apostle Paul said Jesus said it is better to give than receive, while according to our Bible, there is no account of that.)

 Christian ladies studying the Bible.

What Jesus Specifically Says about Our Souls

Personally, I feel some people come back to time and space after they die for whatever reason – maybe to make amends, or for a particular assignment. It also might be only if a person transacted his soul to the dark side and didn't ask for forgiveness before he died; then it's the only way he wouldn't be given another chance to make amends here in time and space.

There are a few verses mentioned by Jesus about the human soul. One that has been mentioned which is, 'For what will it profit a man if he gains the whole world [wealth, fame, Success], but forfeits his soul? Or what will a man give in exchange for his soul?' The second verse would be from Matthew 10:28 – 'Do not be afraid of those who kill the body but cannot kill the soul. Rather be afraid of the One who can destroy both the soul and body in Hell.'

I find the verses interesting, and I would like to elaborate on both of them. As I mentioned before, people perish due to lack of knowledge. It's important that we know the Word written in the Bible. I believe that a lot of people wanted to be successful in their particular fields and felt the only way to realise such aspirations was to make a deal with the dark side and transact their souls; they were ignorant that God promises to bless His people. God's way and timing will certainly be different from ours and might take longer, compared to the quick-fit method from the dark side. But if our souls live forever, why risk where the final destination of our souls reside?

Matthew 8:36 states Jesus used the words *lose* and *forfeit of one's soul*, as well as *in exchange of one's soul*. An individual could use her soul in a transaction. You will be amazed at the number of people who have made the mistake.

There is nothing wrong with material blessing, but it takes an old and matured soul to realise that it's God's way or the highway. The reason is if a person makes a deal with the dark side, then he is owned by the dark side for eternity.

Again, I believe God does bless His people, as He did Father

Abraham. But just as God really tested Abraham, we could expect the same. See Galatians 3:13 – 'That the blessing of Abraham might come on the Gentiles through Jesus Christ; that we might receive the promise of the Spirit through faith.'

This research is about the human soul, so it's my primary objective to stay on the subject matter. Another popular verse of Jesus is from Matthew 10:28, and the end of verse says, 'Rather be afraid of the One who can destroy both the soul and body in Hell.' Here we have Jesus say that a person's soul can be destroyed in hell. There will be a whole chapter based on heaven and also on hell.

Some people don't believe in hell, and some believe they are going straight to hell. I believe that it's never too late to ask for God's mercy and grace; see Luke 22:43. Jesus said to the thief on the cross, 'Truly I tell you, today you will be with me in paradise,' but I need to point out some important factors here. The thief made the first move – he asked Jesus to remember him when Jesus got to his kingdom. We always have to ask and draw near to God, and He will draw near to us. God is faithful like that; it's His nature. Also, there were two thieves on separate crosses, but only one asked for mercy. That tells me it's up to us, and it's our choice. To reiterate, it's never too late. We have to wake up and see the bigger picture. To me personally, it's eternity in paradise, and our souls can live forever.

 Christian girl in prayer. Prayer must pay a large part of the Christian faith – and in fact of any faith. It takes grace to walk on the straight and narrow. Therefore we have to imitate our Lord and Saviour Jesus Christ and pray without ceasing.

Chapter 5

SOME RENOWNED PHILOSOPHERS VIEW THE SOUL

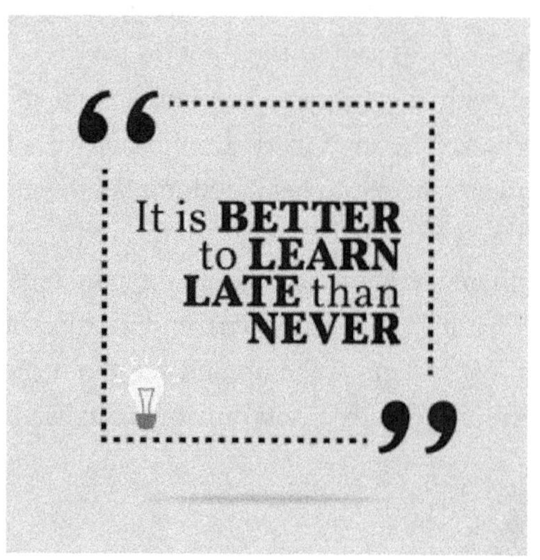

L et's have a look at what a few world-renowned philosophers have to say about the human soul.

Socrates

Socrates was a Greek philosopher and was born in Athens, Greece, in 470 BC. According to biography.com, what we know about Socrates is what has been revealed to us by his students. Plato was his student.

It is stated on biography.com that Socrates believed philosophy should achieve practical results for the greater well-being of society. He pointed out that human choice was motivated by the desire for happiness. Ultimate wisdom comes from knowing oneself. The more a person knows, the greater his or her ability to reason and make choices that will bring true happiness. I agree with the importance of self-awareness, which is basically the pursuit of finding oneself. My saying is, 'We have to find ourselves, and then stay true to the person we have found.' For the most part, we begin to know ourselves after a lot of life experiences.

Socrates believed that even after death, the soul exists and is able to think. He believed that as bodies die, the souls are continually reborn in subsequent bodies. Most religions such as Christianity believe this, as we have seen in the lives of some biblical prophets.

He also had firm hope that something awaits us when we die, and that something was much better for the good than the wicked. This is very much in line with the teachings of the Bible, and I'm sure other religions believe the same concept. Some will use the word Karma; others will say what goes around comes around (**good people get their reward, as mentioned since our actions are recorded, we will reap what we have sown in this life).**

Socrates believed that the human soul was invisible and immortal, and directs the physical body. According to Christian neuroscience, Socrates argued that the soul is what makes a body alive. Death occurs when the soul ceases to animate the body.

To me, the above is pretty obvious, but I also know not everybody agrees with this school of thought. The reason could be due to the age of their souls.

Plato

The next philosopher I would like to introduce is Plato. Plato was a student of Socrates, and he shared similar thoughts as his teacher. He considered the psyche to be the essence (the heart and soul) of a person and makes us behave the way we do. Psyche is the combination of the human mind, both conscious and unconscious. Psychology is the study of the human mind – in other words, the psyche. He agreed with his teacher Socrates that even after death, the soul exists and is able to think. Also, he believed that as bodies die, the soul is reborn into subsequent bodies.

Plato's theory was that the soul consists of three parts.

1. The logos (mind, nous, or reason)
2. The thymos (emotions, spiritedness, or masculine)
3. The eros (appetitive, desire, or feminine)

Plato believes the only part of the soul that is immortal is the logos. He states that these different parts are located in different parts of the body, just as we have different chakras located in specific parts of the body. The logos can be found in the head, helps us with reasoning, and controls other parts of the body and soul. The thymos can be found around the chest area, and it controls anger. The eros can be found around the stomach area and controls desire. He further said the each part's positive output contributes to the well-being of the whole soul.

What Plato believes in is in line with the notion that the soul is a separate entity from the body. People describe the same thing or belief using different terminology, which is fine.

Aristotle

Aristotle saw the soul as the 'first actuality' of a naturally organized body, and he says it's not a separate existence from the physical body. His view is that the primary activity of a living thing constitutes its soul. Before I continue, I must say my thoughts resonate more with Socrates and Plato. I understand where Aristotle is coming from, but I don't agree with his train of thoughts.

Aristotle's views on the human soul are documented in his work *De Anima (On the Soul)*. Unlike Plato, he does not believe in the immortality of the soul. He says living beings are substance and that there are three types of substance.

1. Matter (potentiality)
2. Form (actuality)
3. The compound of matter and form.

He believes that the soul is the form of the body and the sum total of the operations of a human being. He also had the impression that there is a ranking in all living beings, that plants have a vegetable soul, that animals are above plants due to their functions and desires, and that human beings have the highest ranking due to their ability to reason.

He goes on to illustrate his perception of the body and the soul using an analogy of an axe. If an axe were a living being, the metal and the wood would be the body, and the capacity to chop would be the soul. If it can't chop any longer, then it would no longer be an axe. What makes it function is the soul.

Another example Aristotle used is the eye. If the eye were an animal, the ability to see (sight) would be the soul. If the eye could no longer see, then it means it no longer has a soul; it's just an eye in name and can't function. Aristotle believes the body and soul are one and are not separate entities. This is unlike Plato, who believed the body and soul are two different entities. Again, I believe the body and soul are different entities, and therefore I agree with Plato.

According to Aristotle, the soul is the form of a body and can't exist without a body. He believed that the soul dies along with the body. Again, I do not agree with him. I believe even when the body dies, the soul lives on; this is also the teaching of Jesus.

The Difference between the Soul and the Spirit

Let me start with what I believe Spirit to be. We are created in the image of God, and He is spirit. Therefore it's fair to say that our spirit is the divine in us, and it's what helps us be in union with God and the spirit world. Our spirit is what gives us life. When the spirit of a person leaves the person, then technically the person is dead.

The soul is the incorporeal and immortal essence of a person, which is needed for our human experience. Some say our souls are part of our spirit, which is understandable. Our souls also have human experiences. That's why, in my opinion, some people come back, such as John the Baptist. When God said to Jeremiah, 'Before you were in your mother womb I knew you and called you,' I believe what God knew was Jeremiah's soul. The soul has a memory and is ever evolving, and we can know how mature a soul is by the character of an individual. As mentioned in earlier chapters, age is not an indicator of the maturity of a human. Rather, I believe it is character and attitude.

Chapter 6

WHEN DOES THE SOUL LEAVE THE BODY?

When and how the soul leaves the body is not really explained in the Christian faith, and what little is there is vague. From a biblical perspective, when the soul leaves the body, then it's in the presence of the Lord. If the soul is what gives life to the body, then it's fair to say when the body dies, the soul leaves the body.

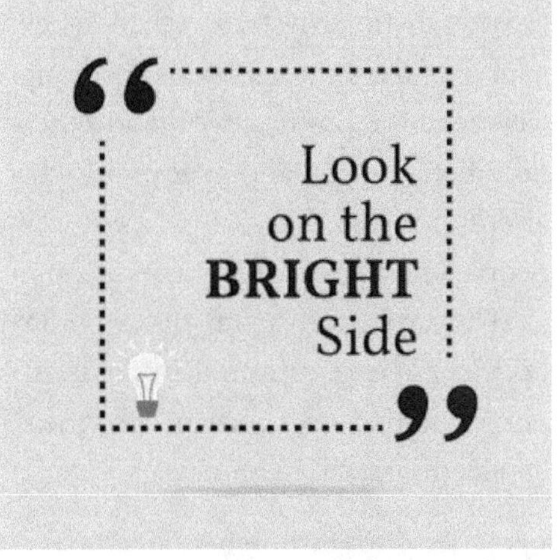

In medical science, they have a term, somatic death, which means the death of the entire body. The person is unconscious, which signifies that communication with the environment is shut down, yet cardiorespiratory function is intact.

It is fair to say that a way to determine whether a person is dead or alive is the withdrawal of artificial maintenance. If a person can't survive upon withdrawal of artificial maintenance, then the person is dead.

I believe that when a person is in a coma, the soul and spirit leave the body and go to the spirit realm. If the individual now wakes up from the coma, then the soul and spirit have obviously come back. As mentioned over and over again, the soul is the life force of any human being. When the soul leaves the body, technically such a person is dead. However, if the person is still breathing by whatever means, time will indicate whether or not such a person's mission is over. As I mentioned earlier, when a person is in coma, I believe the soul is in the spirit world. If there is unfinished business in time and space, then the person will come back to life.

There is a similarity with when we sleep. What happens when we sleep is kind of like a mystery. The soul leaves the body, goes to the spirit world, and comes back as we wake up. Most of the time, we don't recollect our dreams, and I believe it has been designed that way. So many things can only be revealed to us when we leave this physical world. Having said that, I believe some people know more than others in regards to this mystery, which I believe is due to the age of a person's soul. Let's say a total life is made up of 100 per cent between time that we live in the physical world and the spirit world. I have a feeling that our time here in time and space and what we know about life (including the afterlife) is less than 20 per cent of what there is to know. Again, some people know more than others.

The timing of astral disembodiment, in which the spirit leaves the body, has been captured by Russian scientist K. Korotkov (2013), who photographed a person at the moment of his death with a bioelectrographic camera.

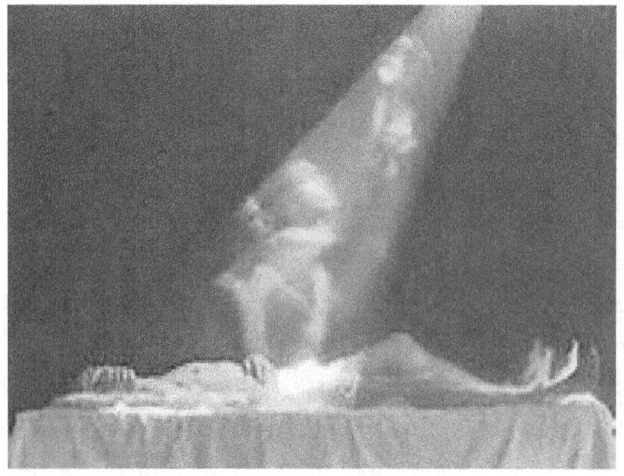

Konstantin Korovin's picture of the soul leaving the body.

The image taken using the gas discharge visualization method, an advanced technique of Kirlian photography, shows in blue the life force of the person gradually leaving the body.

As described in A. Telman's article 'The Soul's Journey from Death to Rebirth', the soul often leaves the body moments before death, when the body is in the greatest pain. The soul then travels through a spiritual passage, which could be depicted as a black tunnel that leads towards the bright white light. This light expands as the soul gets closer to it.

There is a feeling from the soul that it is being pulled towards and into the bright white light. This bright white light is also describe as a golden grey colour, which increases in size as the soul comes closer, and then the soul is pulled in. However, some souls refuse to enter for various reasons. The word *crossover* is seldom used to describe this experience.

The soul that refuses to cross over could be maybe because of a sudden or unexpected death. It could also be unfinished business in time and space, or even fear and confusion.

Basically, when a person dies, for the most part the soul wants to transcend into the spirit realm as soon as possible. However, they do like to stay around and comfort loved ones before finally going into the light.

Time in the physical and in spiritual world is different, and days in the physical realm are like a moment in the spirit world. The spirit realm is also a place that has no time. Therefore a soul could stay around for a 'moment', but in the physical world it could be termed as days. This staying around for a little while could also be for the body lying in rest and all the ceremonies associated with dying.

It's also important to remember that it's only in our world that we experience emotions, so all the sorrow we feel from the result of the loss a loved one, the departed soul, does not feel that way. They have started to see in a different light, aware of the mechanic of life and death, and they know the people they left behind will be seen again. This could be in the spirit world or maybe in another life. The question is how one would know whether one knew someone in a different world.

This is not science, and we can't prove anything, but we do have experiences when we meet some people and really get along, and there is a special bond despite only knowing them for a short while. I strongly feel it's either we, the person in a past life, the spirit world, or fate orchestrating the meeting.

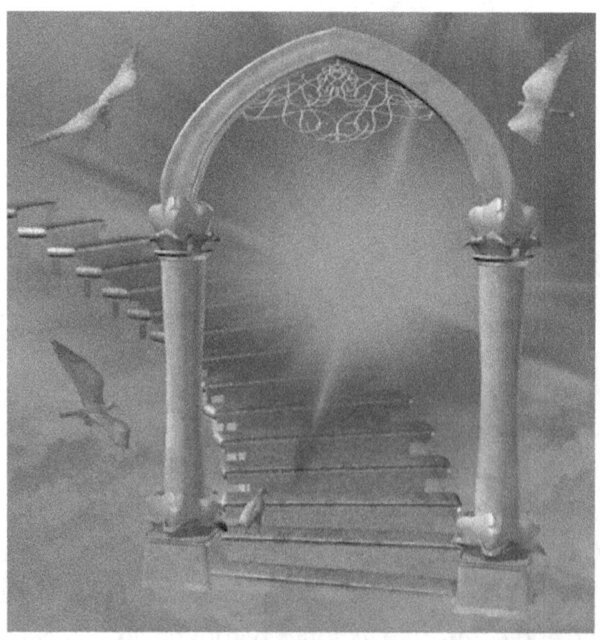

Let's go back to when the soul leaves the body. It feels this gentle pulling into the light. According to Newton (2010), it's a place of love and a feeling of pure, unconditional love, with all negative emotions gone. The stages and the process now begin as we adjust to our home in the spirit world.

The spirit world can be termed as a place of love; however, that depends on the place to which a person goes. I have heard in the past that by looking at a dead person's face, one could indicate the destination in the spirit world. I guess a peaceful face means a good place, and a fearful face could mean an unpleasant destination in the spirit world.

This process is obviously easy and quicker for old souls compared to younger souls, which is understandable. The old soul recollects and remembers the process will go along with hardly any resistance. The things we could not remember or be made aware of will start will start to flood our spirit.

The soul encounters different degrees of brightness as the lights are layered. The lights get brighter as the soul gets closer and enters this light. The layers could be the different spheres in the spirit world. The lights then go from grey to white. It is also said that sometimes the soul will hear sound along the way, which feels like a vibration; this makes the soul feel reinvigorated.

Now the soul is met by familiar faces as a way of welcoming and comforting it. It could also be initially met by its spirit guide, or the spirit guide could stay in the background and approach the soul later. Again, all this depends on the age of the soul and also the experience.

The next stage will be coming from the light and going into a big auditorium, which shines brightly with flashes of light. The soul gravitates towards these flashes of light because they are energies of other souls. The newly arrived soul will be familiar with part of the flashes or energies because they will be people from past lives, or known from the spirit world in the past. The ones closer are the newly arrived souls, and familiar faces will be recognised which could be from past lives, and flashes of light farther away are older souls in the spirit realm.

I believe this because I have had dreams of such auditoriums on two occasions. The first was when my mother passed on. The day she died, before I knew she had died, I had a dream of her going into an auditorium, accompanied by my late father, who'd died thirty-four years before. I was woken up from this dream by my sister to tell me that our mum had passed away. I also had another dream of seeing a world-famous artist sitting in an auditorium, and this artist had died at the time of the dream. I wanted to take a picture of him, and he said I shouldn't.

I believe every sphere will have an auditorium, or something of such nature. I mentioned in earlier chapters that we have seven spheres. I believe we will be pulled into the appropriate sphere. Our spirit guides will assist us in what needs to happen at subsequent stages. Our progression will depend on the conditions of our souls because our lives will be played back to us; it is what religion will call judgement. Again, the word shouldn't be viewed as negative; it is the accumulation of facts to make a decision. This decision indicates the next step or place we go. Even for souls that will go to the kingdom, the celestial sphere, there are different sections that a soul will go.

The primary purpose of a Christian is to be conformed (moulded) into the image of His Son, and this is what leads to oneness with God. Jesus has this oneness, and this is what every Christian has to attain. Jesus said He and His Father are one. Some achieve this before they die, but many Christians don't. This will indicate where we go even in the kingdom. Again, I believe we can grow in the spirit realm. Not everybody is going to be able to hang out in the same place, even in the kingdom.

Chapter 7

WHAT IS HEAVEN?

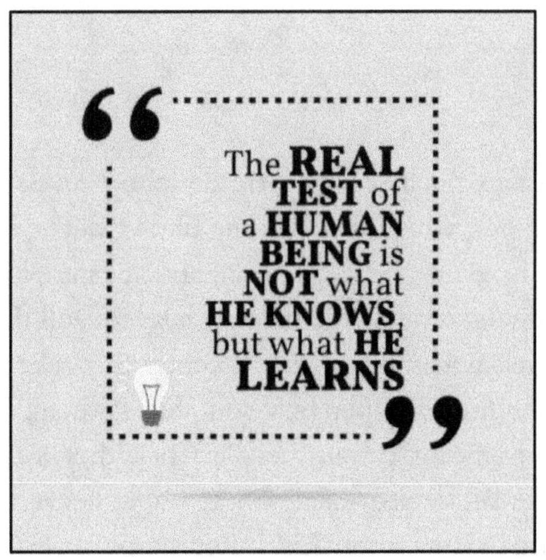

Heaven is the afterlife, the home of God and His angels. It's also known as paradise, or the celestial sphere. Heaven is the place that some people go to after leaving the physical body. Heaven is the eternal home of our spirits and souls. Heavenly beings come to earth, such as Jesus. Some earthly beings will ascend to heaven in the afterlife. Some people have entered heaven alive, such as Elijah and Enoch.

From a Christian perspective, there are three levels of heaven. The first is the firmament, which is where the birds fly. The second heaven is outer space; this is where the sun, moon, and stars are located. The third heaven (according to some) is the seventh heaven, and that is where God and His holy angels and saints dwell. To enter this celestial sphere is not based on the condition of a person's soul, but faith and believe in Jesus. This will be the home of certain people when they leave this time and space reality. The Bible also talks about a new heaven and new earth. This can be found in Revelation 22:17. Revelation21v1

Then I saw 'a new heaven and a new earth,' for the first heaven and the first earth had passed away, and there was no longer any sea. (it's fair to say God knew the Devil would corrupt mankind, and that's why we need a new earth) I saw the Holy City, the New Jerusalem, coming down out of heaven from God, prepared as a bride beautifully dressed for her husband. And I heard a loud voice from the throne saying, 'Look! God's dwelling place is now among the people, and he will dwell with them. They will be his people, and God himself will be with them and be their God.

He will wipe every tear from their eyes. There will be no more death,' or mourning or crying or pain, for the old order of things has passed away.'

He who was seated on the throne said, 'I am making everything new!' Then he said, 'Write this down, for these words are trustworthy and true.'

So how do we as a people make it to this beautiful place? Well, I am going to base this on what I am familiar with, and this is Christianity. The first verse I would like to start with is from the Gospel of Luke. It is chapter 10, starting from verse 26. 'And behold, a certain lawyer stood up and tested Him, saying, "Teacher, what shall I do to inherit eternal life?"' (Eternal **life could be just to reside** in any of the seven spheres. Paradise is what we believe to be the celestial sphere.)

He (Jesus) said to him, 'What is written in the law? What is your reading *of it?*

So he answered and said, 'You shall love the LORD your God with all your heart, with all your soul, with all your strength, and with all your mind,[a] and your neighbour as yourself.'

I really find this verse interesting for several reasons. First, the person was an educated individual who probably had the capacity to reason and intellectualise statements. Second, Jesus asked, 'What is written in the law?' To me, this means that one can find salvation from the Old Testament, because the law is part of the Old Testament, given to Moses from God. Also, I like to point out the word *love*. The greatest power ever will always be love. It also has the highest level of emotional and vibrational frequency. There are other instances when Jesus said to believe in Him and be saved.

I can only talk about what I believe in, and let other people find their own path spiritually. Having said that, one thing all religions should have in common has to be love. We can love our neighbours as ourselves and not hurt our fellow human beings.

Going back to Luke 10:26–27, most people will have no problem loving God, and they may sometimes justify their actions out of love for God. But the verses have two requirements for eternal life, and the second part is loving one's neighbour. I also believe that the scale in the hands of Archangel Michael will be used to measure our love walk in this time and space. Based on the condition of the soul, it will take a soul to any of the seven spheres. Faith in Jesus will take us to the celestial sphere, the kingdom sphere.

As I said, the requirement to enter the celestial sphere is faith in Jesus. However, there is still going to judgement in the house of God (amongst those who believe in Christ). Every action or inaction is a deed, and it's either good or bad. All our deeds are recorded. The late Muhammad Ali did a lot of good deeds even when he was suffering from his illness. His wife said he was doing them as good deeds that would get him to heaven. This is very biblical, as Jesus said in Matthew 6:20–21. 'But store up for yourselves treasures in heaven, where moth and rust do not destroy, and where thieves do not break in and steal. For where your treasure is, there your heart will be also.'

How do we store treasures in heaven? There is no other way apart from our good deeds. Also look at verse 21, which says where your treasure is, there you heart will be also. If we replace *heart* with *soul*, then it equals to where our treasure is in heaven (the more treasure, the higher the place), that is where our souls will go. As I have mentioned earlier, all our actions are recorded in our soul. Even in the kingdom of God, the celestial sphere is a hierarchy.

As I mentioned above about the new heaven and earth, the requirement would be to make it into the current third heaven. I have found interesting that some people assume they are not destined for heaven and think that hell is their final destination. God is rich in mercy, and it's never too late with God to ask for His mercy, no matter what wrong a person might have done in his lifetime. Even if people have made a path with the dark side, ask for mercy and forgiveness, start doing good, and save your soul. Do not be deceived for a second to think this time and place is all there is. Sometimes – in fact, many times recently – my heart and soul are in the spirit world, and it's only my physical body that is here in time and

space. It's a feeling that is so beautiful and peaceful.

Does Hell Exist?

Christianity and Islam believe in the notion of eternal damnation, which is the destination of hell.

Hell was originally created for the Devil and his fallen angels (demons). There was a war in heaven in which the Devil and a third of the angels in heaven rebelled against God. The war in heaven was between the Devil and the angels that were on his side, and Archangel Michael and his angels from heaven. The Devil and his angels lost the battle, and as a result they were kicked out of heaven.

Hell is mentioned in the Old Testament and in the New Testament. However, in the Old Testament, the words such are *hade* and *sheol*. According to Wikipedia, Hades is a Greek word, and the Hebrew translation is Sheol. This place is a place of darkness where the dead go (based on the condition of the soul). Basically, they are cut off from life and God. Hell is also called the lake of fire. According to scriptures, it is the place made for the Devil and his angels. The Bible also says it's a place of eternity that is forever and ever, where those that dwell in such place will be tormented and will be in anguish day and night. Christianity teaches that accepting Jesus Christ as Lord will help us escape this dark and horrible place. Also, Jesus said in Luke 10:26 that by loving God with all we have, and by loving our neighbour as ourselves, it will grant us eternal life, which means a place in heaven (this could mean the second to seventh spheres).

I ponder on the thought that maybe good and decent people will

default and make heaven, even if they have no religious background. Some later research showed that they will be judged based on the condition of their souls and will go to one of the spheres. Maybe this is where the scale of Archangel Michael will come into place and measure their deeds during a person's lifetime. Another school of thought is that if a person is good and decent, the individual will not go to hell but maybe not to heaven either. They could end up in one of the spheres.

As Christians who have the Holy Spirit living in them, those who make a pact with the Devil and sell their souls will have demons in them. Unless they get rid of such darkness before they die, I don't think heaven will be their destiny. Again, later research showed that they will go to the first sphere, which is a place of darkness. The good news is the moment they accept the light and ask for God's mercy, I sincerely believe God will forgive and grant mercy.

The funny thing is people in darkness believe they are in the light, and that Lucifer is the light. If that is the case, how come he was locked out and kicked from heaven? I'll leave that one for you to figure out.

What Souls Go to Hell

Based on what is said in the scriptures, hell is a place made for the Devil and his angels (demons). When human beings make a pact with the dark side, some of them possess a demon, and because the demon's final destination is in hell, so will the individual go. It's called eternal damnation. The fact also is the new heaven promised by God will only be for those who believed in Jesus and made Him their Lord and Saviour.

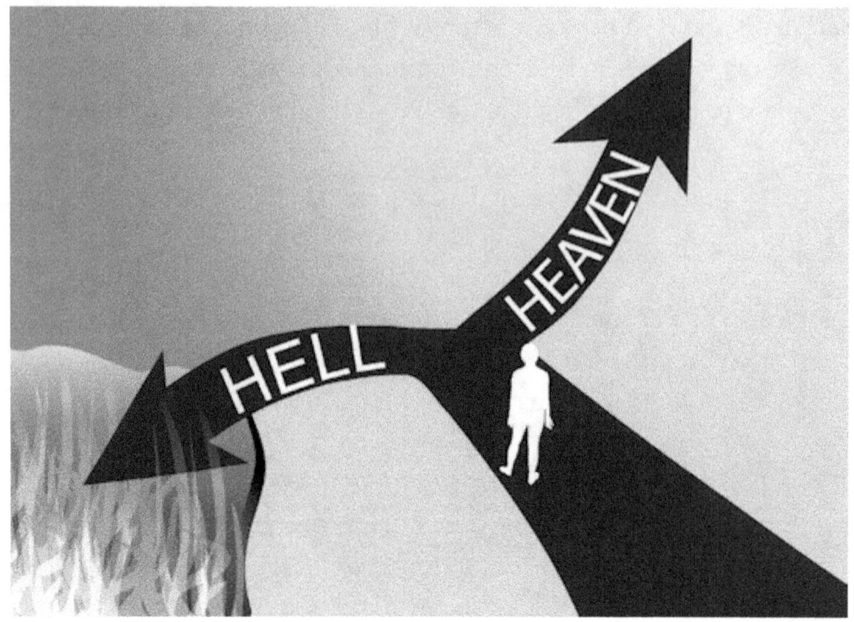

Another way of looking at it is when people sell their souls, their new boss is now in total control of their lives. In return for this exchange of individuals' souls is diabolical favours. Such favours could be knowledge, wealth, fame, or power.

I believe that's why Jesus said in Mark 8:36, 'For what shall it profit a man, if he gains the whole world and lose his own soul?' It's fair to say that a person's soul is lost when it can't make it to heaven. If the individual's new master can't make it to heaven, it would take a miracle for the person who sold her soul to make heaven. However it's possible to make amends and renounce the Devil and his kingdom. Simply be prepared for a good fight in the spirit world, also known as spiritual warfare.

Matthew 4:8 says the Devil showed Jesus all the kingdoms of the world, and all the great things that are in those kingdoms. The Devil then said to Jesus, 'If you bow down and worship me, I will give you all these things.' Jesus said to the Devil, 'Go away from me, Satan. It is written you must worship the Lord your God and serve Him only.'

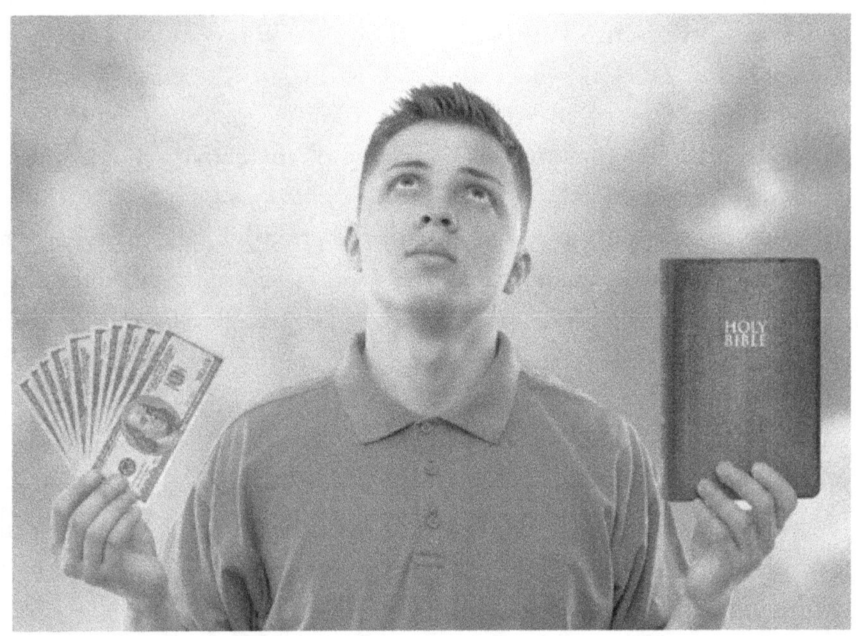

God dwells in heaven, and in order for us to gain entry, we must serve God only. It's interesting to see what's going around nowadays. Even in a lot of Christian gatherings, the name of Jesus is proclaimed, but these places are mixing and using power from other sources. That's why in Matthew 7:23, Jesus said He will say to them openly (publicly), 'I never knew you, depart from Me … you who act wickedly.' Jesus also said, 'Many will say on that day, Lord, Lord did we not prophesy in Your name, cast out demons in Your name, perform many miracles? And I then I will declare to them, I never knew you; Depart from Me, you who practise lawlessness.'

First, let's look at the words *many miracles*. A place that performs many miracles could have a large following, but we shouldn't be fooled by the large crowd, because the Bible says we have to test the spirit. Many miracles could also indicate a famous name. Again, we shouldn't be fooled. A lot of so-called Christian places practise a lot of witchcraft, mind-control activities, chanting, incarnations, enchantments on people to come to their gatherings, and appearing in people's dreams to manipulate them. This is definitely not of God. In Matthew 7:23, Jesus said, 'You who practise Lawlessness. If you break the law of Love you break the law of God because God is Love.' Therefore practising witchcraft, mind control, and various forms of magic is stealing energy from people. **Basically if a person feels convicted of any activity that is not of God, stop.**

The temptation is that humans want the good life, and they want it now. People are not willing to wait for God's blessing, and ultimately God owns everything. God's primary objective is the development of our souls, and that is the main reason why we came to this time and space reality.

From Abraham, David, and Joseph, all eventually receives what we term as the good life, but we also see the process they had to endure. One of the reasons for such drilling is to mature our souls. I feel we can grow and mature our souls in both the spirit and physical world, but I don't have the answer to what determines where we grow.

Yes, we know the Devil and his fallen angels still have some power, and they have the ability to give humans whatever they want. But are they worth the exchange of our souls?

I mentioned in an earlier chapter that we are in different stages of soul development. There are some mystical things that we know in our hearts, or that have been revealed to us. I believe for us to simply know something means our souls know it for previous life experiences. That's why I believe matured and old souls will have the least percentage of soul selling.

Chapter 8

RELIGION'S PERCEPTION OF HEAVEN AND HELL

What I find fascinating in this time and space reality is that there are certain topics and subjects on which we agree, and some on which we are divided. We agree more about natural and secular things, but we are divided on spiritual matters, and we have various views and perceptions about the afterlife. Why is this?

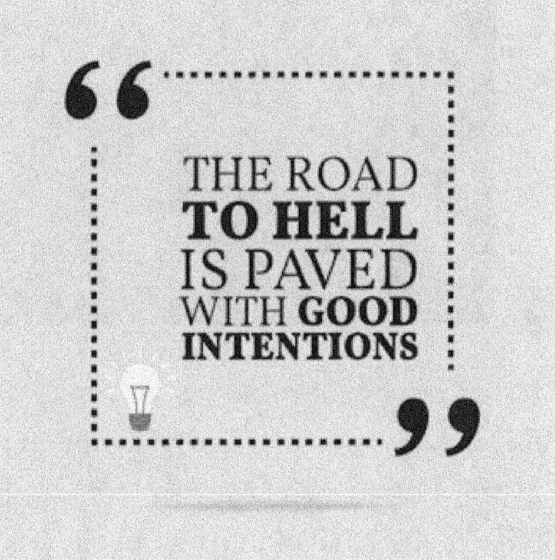

If we believe for the most past that there is one God, should there not be one truth? We all have to find the truth for ourselves and not be forced, tricked, or manipulated to believe something. What does not resonate with our consciousness, we should do away with – it's as simple as that.

I strongly feel we go to different places in the spirit world when we die. I don't think our minds can comprehend the spirit world, and I believe it has been done deliberately. However, what gave me some form of insight is a quote from Jesus in the Gospel of John.

In My Father's house are many dwelling places. If it were not so, I would have told you, because I am going there to prepare a place for you. And if I go and prepare a place for you, I will come back again and I will take you to Myself, so that where I am you may be also. And [to the place] where I am going, you know the way.' Thomas said to Him, 'Lord, we do not know where You are going; so how can we know the way?' Jesus said to him, '[a]I am the [only] Way [to God] and the [real] Truth and the [real] Life; no one comes to the Father but through Me. (John 14:2–6)

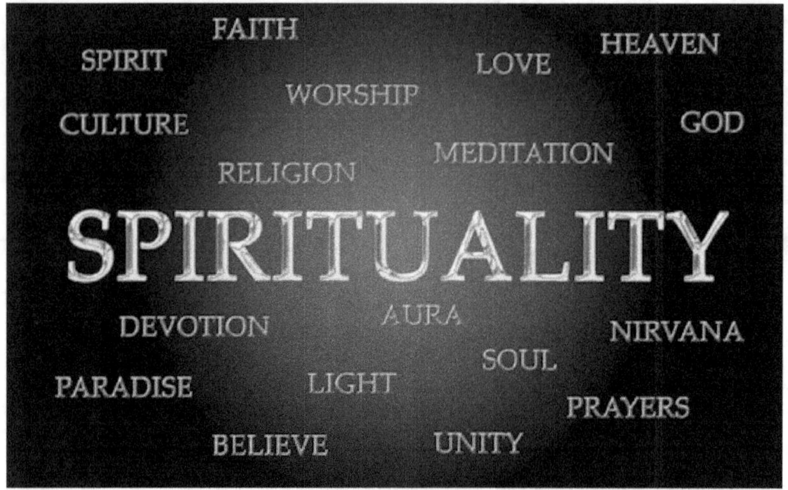

Let me break these verses down analytically. The phrase *dwelling place* also means houses; other versions use the word *mansions*. We have to be careful not to perceive it as we would something in the natural world. What is the revelation of what He was saying Looking further, Jesus said, 'I am going to prepare a place for you.' We could say it's a special area for Jesus's folks, right? Don't forget He said there are many dwelling places. The word *many* means amounting to or consisting of a large, indefinite number. Basically, the size of the spirit is beyond our wildest imagination. Jesus then said, 'I am coming to get you and take you to Myself, so where I am you will be also.' We have established how huge heaven is, and Christians will obviously be in Jesus's corner. What about the many more corners, dwelling places, houses, and mansions? Who dwells in them?

Jesus said, 'The place I am going you will know.' Thomas said, 'How will we know where you are going if we do not know the way?' Jesus said, 'I am the way the real truth and the real life and no one comes to the

Father but through Me.' I am the way, the truth, and the life. No one comes to the Father except through Me.(John 14.4-6)

To me, this is saying for a Christian, the way to the Father is through Jesus. But let's not forget He also said in His Father's house, where are many mansions and dwelling places. Who is going to occupy the other mansions and dwelling places?

So let's look at various religions and see their take on heaven.

Judaism

The Jews are people God called to Himself. In other words, they are God's own people. They are still waiting for the arrival of their Messiah, because they don't believe Jesus is the Messiah. The two main sects are the Pharisees and the Sadducees. The Pharisees believe in the afterlife, whereas the Sadducees don't believe in the afterlife, citing there's no biblical evidence to suggest the existence of such. There holy book is called the Torah, which is the first five books of the Bible. Most of them believe that there is going to be a Day of Judgement. A vast majority of them believe in the afterlife, and the Israelites are very religious and hold fast to their rich heritage of Father Abraham and the laws God gave to Moses.

Christianity

Christianity believes in heaven and also expects a new heaven and new earth, as written in the Book of Revelation. Christians believes in the Lord Jesus Christ as Lord and Saviour. Faith in Jesus, according to the Bible, indicates a believer's name should then we written in the Lamb's book of life. In the occurrence of this, eternal life is granted. Basically there is nothing we can do to earn it; it's simply faith in Jesus, accepting Him as Lord and Saviour.

Islam

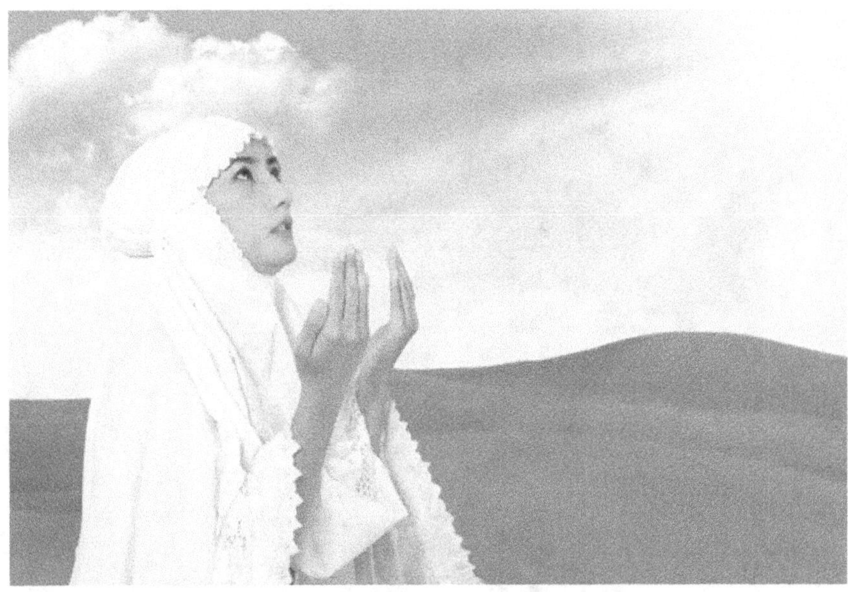

In Islam, heaven is referred to as paradise, and those whose good works outweighed their bad will go to paradise (condition of the soul). The good works are obeying Allah's laws. They feel if they follow the teachings of Mohammed, then they will go to heaven. Obviously, a lot of people will question recent activities done in the name of this religion, as well as the fact that they do it in the name of Allah. On the other hand, people like the late Muhammad Ali, a man people loved round the world, was a Muslim and said the religion is about love and peace.

God is love and is a spirit, and if we are made in the image of God, which is love, then our acts should be of love if we have the Spirit of God in us. It's obvious that people have different spirits in them, and by our acts, we shall know what spirit is in us. Whoever does not love does not know God, because God is love.

Buddhism

Buddhism refers to heaven as Nirvana, a place where the spirit is joined with God. To get to Nirvana – a blissful, transcendental, high level of consciousness and a spiritual state – a person must follow an eightfold path. This includes understanding the universe, as well as speaking and acting in the appropriate manner. Upon the diligent practice of the required steps, one would unite one's spirit to God.

The above is similar to what Jesus said: 'I and my Father are one.' Jesus also prayed that His followers would be one in them (Jesus and God). To be one with God is a place we grow into in the spirit; it's not just getting to this place, but maintaining that place in the spirit. For the continuous attainment of oneness, it would require a balance between challenges and the glory that results from the oneness. To keep us on our toes, God will allow some unpleasant things to happen, though not to overcome us. The more we keep close to Him, the more we know spiritually, and the more persecution will come to us. We see the same pattern in Paul's life, the 'thorn in the flesh' scenario, so that he would be exalted beyond measure. I see this in my life: I get revelations from God, and I think, 'Yes, If I operate and do somethings in a certain way, then no more attacks, all I will experience is peace, but what I have realised God allows the attacks to keep us on point and spiritually hot and not lukewarm.

I believe that's how we maintain the oneness with God. Spiritual truth is parallel, and the principles are similar. The difference is that we call upon different deities.

Taoism

In the beginning Taoism did not put must emphasis in the afterlife and focused on the creating a utopian society, a community or society that in theory possesses highly desirable or nearly perfect qualities. Salvation to them is to be achieved by aligning with cosmos and receiving aid from supernatural beings that lived on mountains and islands. However, they have now embraced the teachings of Buddhism in regards to the afterlife.

Hinduism

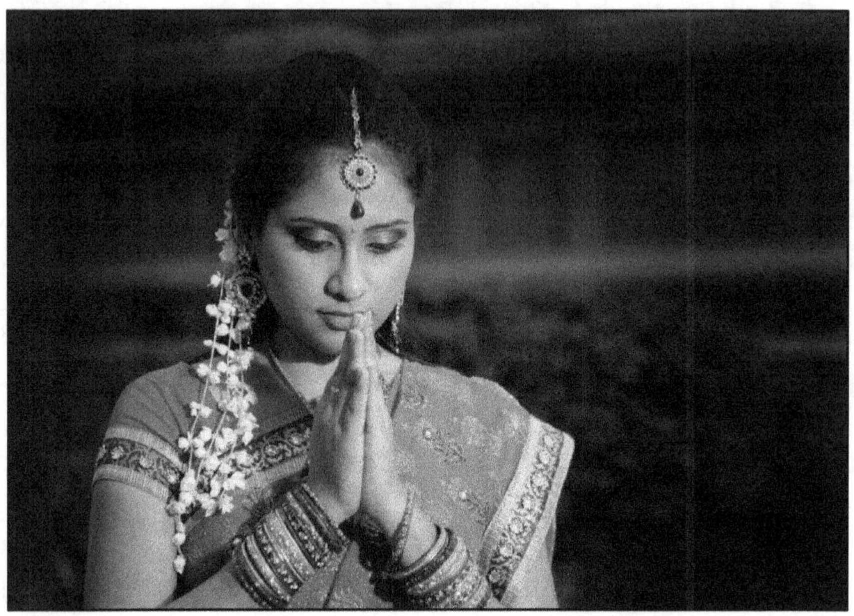

According to Hinduism, after a person has lived out the cycle of reincarnation, then the spirit can be in union with God. The cycle of reincarnation would be ridding the soul of bad karma and evil actions. This they say can be done in three ways: by selfless devotion and service to a particular god, by understanding the nature of the universe, and by mastering the actions to fully please the gods.

In Hinduism, it is said they have many gods, in the millions. After a while, a person finds what is right for him in terms of spiritual paths. Discipline and dedication are important for growth to occur. We should be in a place where we can flow in spirit and truth with God, and not need a third party or middle person before we can talk to God.

Chapter 9

WHY ARE WE HERE?

I believe that there is only one truth, and if we can agree that there is one way, we come to earth, time and space, which is through a woman's womb. Then we should be able to agree in the one truth that happens to us when we die. As I have mentioned earlier, my faith is Christianity. I believe in Jesus as my Lord, the power of His name, and why he came.

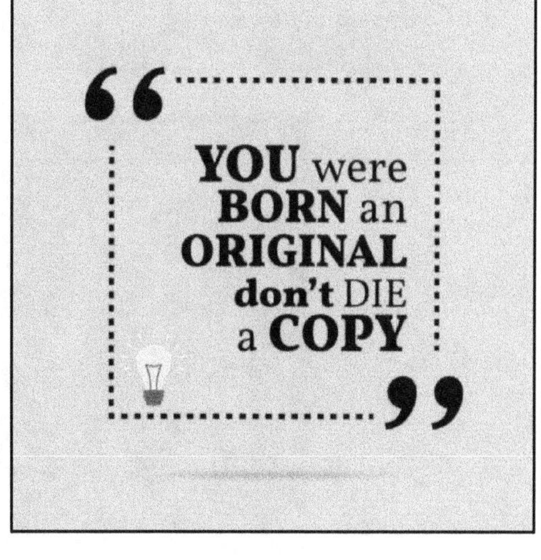

I believe that Jesus was the light that came and still is the light, and the Light shines on in the darkness, for the darkness has never overpowered it (John 1:5). Having said that, I don't want to be seen as religious, and I don't follow the crowd. The truth has to be revealed to me.

The primary reason why we are here is to grow our souls and get it closer to wholeness or oneness with God. The second or secondary reason we are here is to help and love each other. This is what I personally believe. As God knew and approved of Jeremiah's soul, likewise myself.

 Prophet Jeremiah.

I am not here to judge others' spiritual beliefs. I am here to help and love my fellow humans, regardless of their spiritual or religious beliefs. If my opinion is asked, then I will voice it. If not, I can simply love and appreciate the people I come across. One of the greatest pains I have faced in life came from religion, and I have learnt my lesson and now know better. We are all on a journey, and it's life's lesson and experiences that teach us.

As a Spirit-filled spiritual Christian, not a religious Christian, the Holy Spirit reveals things to me, and it is later confirmed through the Word (Bible). In most cases, I have found it's the reading between the lines, or it can be confirmed through a person, circumstance, or someone else's writing.

Our primary teacher is the Holy Spirit, and let's looks at some verses: 1 John 2:27 (King James Version). 'But the anointing which ye have received of him abideth in you, and ye need not that any man teach you: but as the same anointing teacheth you of all things, and is truth, and is no lie, and even as it hath taught you, ye shall abide in him.'

Look at the second line of this verse. It says that we need not any man teaches us but the Holy Spirit ill teach us all things. So it's either we rely on the Holy Ghost, as I like to put it (ghost and spirit mean the same thing) to teach us, or we down grade and fall short to religion. I don't know about your experience, but my experience, as I mentioned earlier, was painful.

I like the Amplified Version of the same verse, so let's have a look.

As for you, the anointing [the special gift, the preparation] which you received from Him remains [permanently] in you, and you have no need for anyone to teach you. But just as His anointing teaches you [giving you insight through the presence of the Holy Spirit] about all things, and is true and is not a lie, and just as His anointing has taught you, [a]you must remain in Him [being rooted in Him, knit to Him].

The line I want to focus on here is where it says the anointing giving us insight through the Holy Spirit. Revelation is another word for insight, and when I read the Bible, that's what I am looking for. I also like to call it reading between the lines.

Again, we are here to grow our souls and help each other. Well, that's why I am here. I know I am an old soul, and I know that God has approved of me. Therefore I am not seeking man's approval (as religion seeks).

Going back to the soul and our reason for being here (pilgrimage), as I have mentioned is to grow our souls so we can ultimately get to that place of wholeness. The Bible verse that comes to mind is 1 John 3:2 (Amplified). 'Beloved, I pray that in every way you may succeed *and* prosper and be in good health [physically], just as [I know] your soul prospers [spiritually].' The word *prosper* comes from the Latin word *prosperare,* which means 'cause to succeed, render happy'(Online Etymology Dictionary). A soul can succeed by walking in love, and the definition of love can be found in 1 Corinthians 13:4–8.

Love endures with patience and serenity, love is kind and thoughtful, and is not jealous or envious; love does not brag and is not proud or arrogant. It is not rude; it is not self-seeking, it is not provoked [nor overly sensitive and easily angered]; it does not take into account a wrong endured. It does not rejoice at injustice, but rejoices with the truth [when right and truth prevail]. Love bears all things [regardless of what comes], believes all things [looking for the best in each one], hopes all things [remaining steadfast during difficult times], endures all things [without weakening]. Love never fails [it never fades nor ends].

I sincerely believe with a lifestyle from the above verse, one's soul will prosper, but inasmuch or eternal benefit, it takes a real enlightened and an awaken soul to get the insight and revelation of this. Old souls would be able to comprehend this faster and easier, but even old souls have to go through valleys for them to really find who they are. For the most part, it happens after the first part of their lives, when they can allow the Holy Spirit be their real and only teacher.

As I have mentioned, we came to time and space to prosper and grow our souls. To do this, our love emotion has to be worked on. If we look at the Old Testament, it's fair to say God gave them the requirements needed to live a life of love. The commandments were a guide to help people live a life of love. As Jesus also said, 'These two commandments, sum up and upon them depend all the Law and the Prophets.' The two commandments are loving God and our neighbours as ourselves.

Chapter 10

NEAR-DEATH EXPERIENCE

onsideration to add is the notion that we are more that our physical images. In this chapter, I want to share various stories of people who went to the other side and came back to tell the stories. Some died, went unconscious, and went to different dimensions. Another way to put it was their souls or spirits left their bodies and went

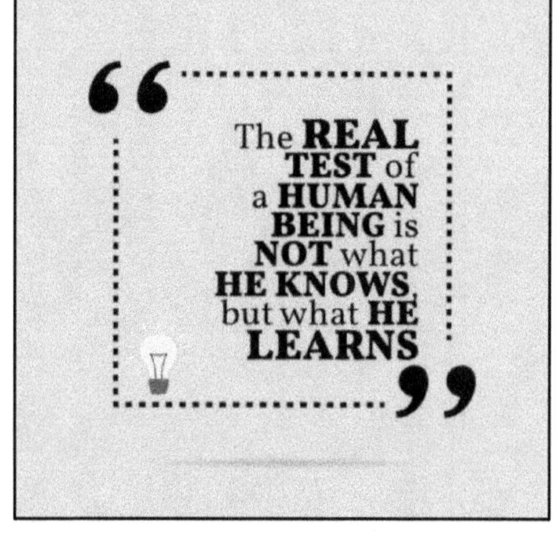

to the ultimate destination. However, it must have not been their time, and that's why they came back. We are fortunate to hear their stories.

The first story is from an accident of Mickey Robinson. He had a fatal accident from an aircraft, and he sustained serious injuries and major burns as a result of the accident. His story (in 'Have You Ever Thought about Your Eternity', no date) talks about how his inner man, his spirit, sat up out of his body. He described it as how a person would take a glove off a hand, and how he was instantly in the spirit world. He said the place was so real, and he used the phrases the real world and the real him.

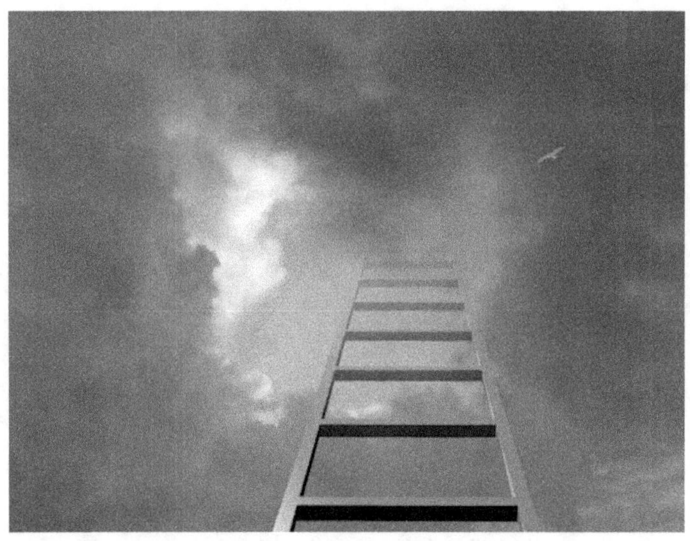

He further says he could see a bright light, and he felt a pull. He had the feeling that he was travelling. This is completely in line to other stories I have read about how people describe the death process.

What makes his story different is that he describes that at his right side, he could feel something, and what he saw was blackness sweeping. The more he looked, the faster it would sweep with great intensity, and he felt cut off from the light. Mickey called this place horrific, and it was also real – a place he was seeing and feeling. The place was closing in on him (the first sphere?). This he believed was hell. On the verge of external separation, he said he screamed out of his spirit, 'I'm sorry. I want to live! Give me another chance!' Before the door closed, he was standing in the presence of God. Mickey said God revealed to him that the darkness he saw was an historical record of his life and the years he lived (the condition of the soul). This takes my mind to the scale in Archangel Michael's hand, which I mentioned in an earlier chapter. God gave him a second chance, and an opportunity to cry out to Him. To summarise his story, it's fair to say that the life we live in time and space will determine where we go when we leave this earth. It also seems that Jesus is an insurance policy to get to the good place, which is heaven. The celestial sphere is not based on the condition of the soul, but on faith in Jesus Christ.]

As told by Reynolds (2015, p. 66), there's also the story of Ellen. She was in a car accident and was in a serious condition. While she was in the hospital, she felt a peaceful presence enter her room and tell her it could be all right if she wanted to let go. Ellen listened to that advice and let go, especially considering the horrific injuries she had sustained from the accident. Ellen was instantly in another place without a body, as a point of light. Another light appeared and pulled her in. She was now surrounded by millions of other lights, as if she was at home. She also felt loving presence next to her, and it was at that point she decided to return home to tell her story. What Ellen experienced is similar to other stories I have mentioned in this book and read elsewhere.

The next story is from the Bible, and it's one from the apostle who wrote 75 per cent of the New Testament. It's not surprising that Paul had a near-death experience. I actually expected it to be more than one recorded incident. Having said that, it is not explicit in the text, but as I always say, you have to read between the lines.

This great apostle was beaten and left for dead on several occasions. His life was at risk after his Damascus experience. In 2 Corinthians 12:4, he mentioned how he was caught up into paradise, and he heard unspeakable words that were not lawful for a man to utter.

This could have resulted from the many incidents he encountered for spreading the Gospel; people everywhere wanted him dead. Going off the topic for a second, anybody who wants to bring light into this world gets attacked by the kingdom of darkness. Well, Jesus said, 'Upon this rock I will build my church and the gates of hell will not prevail against it.'

Celebrities Who Had Near-Death Experiences

As described by Bauer (2011, p. 310) a few celebrities had near-death experiences. One thing I have noticed is that all the descriptions of a NDE are very similar for both people of faith and otherwise. They all come to the realisation that what they underwent was so real, even more real than our earth's time and space.

The first is Ozzy Osbourne, who stopped breathing after a bike accident and was in coma. He described an experience of seeing a bright light that emerged from darkness. The incident in his words made him come to terms with his life and grow up.

The next celebrity is Jane Seymour, who suffered from a bad flu and was given some form of medication to which she was allergic. Her situation got worse, she was rushed to hospital, and she probably went unconscious. She describes how she left her body, looked around, and saw herself lying in bed. She watched the doctors try to resuscitate her. While out of her body, she moved to the top corner of her room, floated above them, and watched as the medical staff pinned her body to the bed and put needles in her arm.

She also remembered her life flash before her eyes, and she wanted to be alive so that she could raise her children. Then she said, 'God, if you are there and really exist, and I survive, I will never use your name in vain again.' She actually died for thirty seconds and then found herself in her body as she woke up.

Sharon Stone had a similar experience when she also had a medical condition. She says how she saw a giant vortex of white light. She narrates it as bright white light, and she started to see some of her friends. As she found herself back in the room, in her body, she describes the events as being an incredible meaningful and important moment of her life.

Finally, we have Gary Busey. The successful Hollywood actor was in the hospital on the operating table. He found himself in another dimension surrounded by angels. He narrates in his biography that the angels were big balls of light that carried with them nothing but warmth and love of an unconditional nature. The occurrence changed his life. He is now a Christian, and Jesus Christ is the Lord of his life. According to Wikipedia, in 1996 Busey publicly announced that he was a Christian, saying, 'I am proud to tell Hollywood I am Christian,' and for the first time he was free to be himself. Gary Busey's NDE has transformed him into a God- fearing man.

I heard something perhaps quoted by St Augustine: 'For God to change a man, He has to appear to a man.' We see this happen to the apostle Paul.

Chapter 11

HOW TO MAKE SURE YOUR SOUL WILL END UP IN HEAVEN

There are so many religions in the world today, but there are spiritual principles that apply to everybody, just like the law of gravity. No one can ever have all the answers, but if we seek revelation and insight, it can be revealed to us. As a spiritual Christian, I believe in the divinity of God the father; Jesus Christ, God the Son; and God the Holy Spirit. I have learned my lessons from religion, and one has to be careful in these last days. A lot of deception is out there, and we need to open our eyes. It's time we focus on a personal relation with God via Jesus Christ.

Following religion and man is more dangerous now that ever. A lot of so-called Christians have sold out, and it's time to watch and pray. Not all those who call Lord will enter the kingdom of God. It is written that in the last days, even the elect will be deceived.

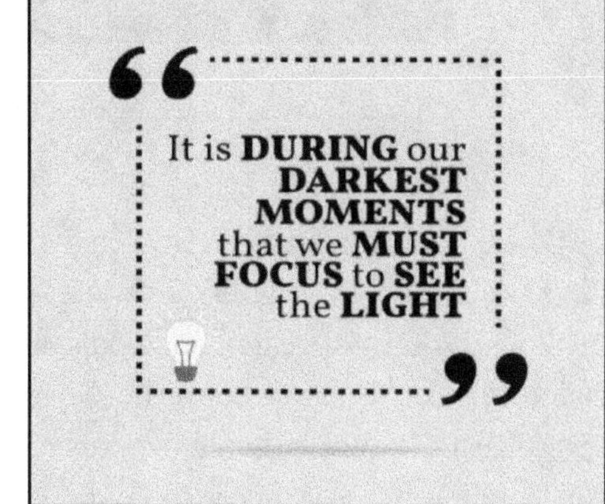

When we answer to God on that day, we are going to do it alone. We have to work out our salvation and not follow the crowd, instead knowing God deep in our hearts. We will mess up and makes mistakes, but God is faithful and will forgive us when we confess our wrongdoings and mistakes.

Only Jesus, not our works, can save our souls, from a Christian's point of view. However, our works of love could determine our location in heaven. We all have a responsibility to draw near to God, and He draws near to us. I wonder how many people go to the spirit world every day; the good thing is we can decide in which part of the spirit world we will end up.

We know there are two kingdoms in our universe, light and darkness. Heaven is light, and the kingdom of darkness will ultimately be hell, the lake of fire according to the Bible. There are seven spheres and a celestial sphere.

 By God's grace, may we always be the light. Amen.

Love is the only way to heaven – by the love we give out and by the love we receive. If we go to Jesus's teaching, He said we should love God with all our minds, hearts, and souls, and we should love our neighbours as ourselves. Also, we see in the Gospel of John that God so loved the world that He sent his only begotten Son, that whoever believes in Him shall not die but have everlasting life (John 3:16).

The requirement for entry into heaven is loving God with all our being. According to Romans 3:23, we all have fallen short of the magnitude that we are supposed to love. In order to make this right, we are graced with John 3:16.

If we look at the definition of love in 1 Corinthians 13, it states that love is patient and kind, does not envy, does not boast, is not rude, is not self-seeking, is not easily angered, and keeps no record of wrong. It's clear to see how any human being would easily fall short of such glory.

Because we could not live up to God's standard, the remedy is John 3:16. This is not by works but by faith. All **and that's why I accept** such generosity, as I cannot live up to God's standards.

Chapter 12

SYNAGOGUE OF SATAN

When Elijah said to God that he was alone and that they sought his life, God told him that He had reserved seven thousand men who had not bowed down to the image of Baal.

Sadly, in our society today, a lot of so-called believers have bowed down. What I find very disturbing is that fact that they

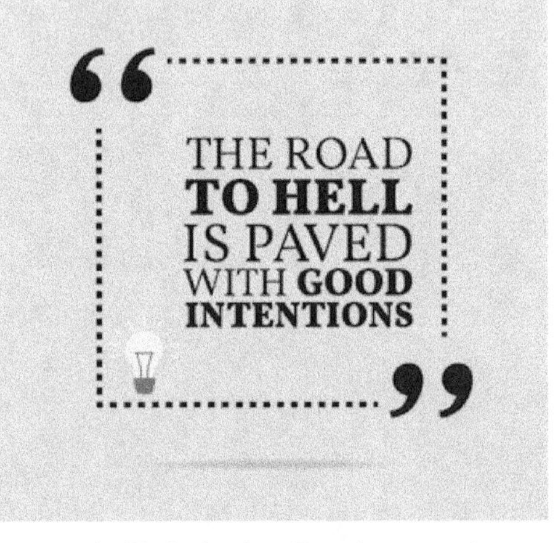

then hide behind the name of Jesus and Christianity. Precious souls are obviously at risk, and a lot of people are genuinely seeking God, but as a result of what is b

een offered, they could end up receiving something else. All I can say is that I am confident that God's grace will help the innocent and make a way of escape at the appropriate time.

It is not just places of worship, but also Christian TV and Christian music. What was supposed to be pure has been polluted.

We saw the same pattern in the Old Testament, over and over again. The truth of the matter is that the idolatry practiced then, thousands of years ago, is going on today. A lot of innocent people are seeking God, but they are deceived because they don't have a clue of what is going on. Having a personal relationship with the Lord is what we hear when we first become Christians. It's more important now than ever.

The reason is simple: we have to train ourselves to hear the voice of the Holy Spirit, because the middle person you are listening to, be it music or messages, might be the one Jesus will say, 'Wicked person, I do not know you.' As a result, a lot of people are being led astray.

From my experience, what keeps helping me is the Holy Spirit. As a result of the deception and lies I have seen in some religious gatherings, I will say bluntly that I trust no one but the Holy Spirit to direct me and talk to me.

One of my favourite verses is 1 John 2:26–27.

These things I have written to you with reference to those who are trying to deceive you [seducing you and leading you away from the truth and sound doctrine]. As for you, the anointing [the special gift, the preparation] which you received from Him remains [permanently] in you, and you have no need for anyone to teach you. But just as His anointing teaches you [giving you insight through the presence of the Holy Spirit] about all things, and is true and is not a lie, and just as His anointing has taught you,[c] you must remain in Him [being rooted in Him, knit to Him].

Anointing is-the power of God, which can be amplified and comes on us by the Holy Spirit. The more sensitive we are to this gift, the more clarity we will find in our decisions. I personally will listen to anybody, but let the Holy Spirit teach me. As the verse says above, the anointing teaches us about all things – not just a few things, but *all* things.

From this gift we are given insight and revelation. God is always speaking and didn't stop the Book of Revelation. God speaks to us for the most part through the Holy Spirit. We don't need to force ourselves to hear; it comes with a bit of cultivating and training oneself to hear.

The problem we have today is that everybody is talking and has something to say. It's like people want to be the junior Holy Spirit, but what they are trying to do is manipulate people. Sadly, religious settings are very big on this. If anything doesn't resonate with us, we shouldn't force it or receive it. Remember, the Holy Spirit teaches us all things will bring whatever we need to know or learn in ways that we can understand. In situations when we miss it, He will bring it back.

With the gift of the Holy Spirit, we can rely on Him telling us where to go and what to listen to. Peace is an indicator of things being of the Holy Spirit. If we don't feel peace about a person, situation, or whatever, we should pause and not do anything.

My spiritual journey has been from the Catholic Church to the Church of England (Anglican) to the Pentecost church, and back to the Catholic Church. People tend to question their doctrines, but they feel comfortable and peaceful going there.

The Holy Spirit will give us individual doctrines based on the word on God, depending on our individual journeys and assignments. Doctrine is defined as act of teaching or what is taught. If by having a personal relationship with the Holy Spirit, He teaches us all things, then we can call the act of His teaching our personal doctrine. Some people have peculiar spiritual journeys and obstacles they have to overcome. Personally, what I have had to overcome has been with the help of the Holy Spirit and not from gathering certain doctrines.

Now I can say I am happy it's worked out that way, because I am not dependant on flesh but on the arm of God.

 Let your light shine. Let's make it better for the next generation. Amen.

The Book of Life

The book of life is basically, a book that has all the names of people that will go to heaven in the afterlife. It is believed to have been written before the foundation of the earth. It might be hard to comprehend with the natural mind, but God already knows those who will inherit the Kingdom of Heaven.

That's why Jesus said no one can come to Him, unless the Father draws the person. This can be found in the sixth Chapter of the gospel of John. In the next two chapters of the same Gospel of John, chapter 8, Jesus said you are of your Father the Devil.

So these Chapters tell us that God has His Children and the devil also has his children. I really believe this to be true. Some say we are all Children of God; such statement is so far from the truth. I have worked with people who do not believe in God a bit. They know there is something about a Child of God, and they would try and steal the anointing of God and the virtues from the child of God, but they don't want anything to do with God. They believe in spirits, and use the Ouija board, but no to God and complete no to Jesus. I have spoken to people who say they believe in the devil but don't believe in God.

The spirits that they get in touch with using things like the Ouija board are fallen angels, demon also known as familiar spirits, all these foul spirits are destined to the abyss and the pits of hell, and the devil is their master.

The point am trying to make is that there is the Kingdom of Heaven, God is the head, and He is our Father and our name should be in the book of life. However we have to work out our salvation with fear and trembling as mentioned in the book of Philippians, in other words make sure that our names are not blotted out of the book. When people say saving of souls, it's basically to help get a person's name written in the book of life.

This concept or term "book of life" can be found in both the old and the New Testament. For instance in the Book of Daniel in the seventh Chapter, Daniel mentions thousand thousands minster to unto Him, and ten thousand times ten thousand stood before him, and the Judgement was set and the books were opened.

I have mentioned in earlier Chapters that everything we do in life is recorded. The Kingdom of God, has a perfect system in keeping records, un like the imperfections that we see in this world. Again the Kingdom of heaven is a place of Justice.

In as much as some people's Father at the minute might be the devil, the have the choice and free will to abandon their current father and chose God as their new Father. God will always welcome people with open and loving hands, regardless of what the person has done in the past. God is rich in mercy like that.

In the New Testament, Jesus sent out 70 disciples, and they performed various sorts of miracles and they came out rejoicing, and saying that spirits were subject to them, Jesus said what they should really be happy about is the fact that their names are written in Heaven.

Apostle Paul has also aware of the book of Life, as he mentioned fellow – labourers in the gospel, whose name were in the book of life.

From a Christian perspective, to get one's name written in this book is Faith in Jesus, and by His grace following His commandments.

In the book of revelations, it states that anyone whose name is not found in the book of life, such person is cast into the lake of fire. Who in their right mind would want to be cast in to the lake of fire?, obviously no one. But the devil has deceived the most of the world. As a result many people can't see and they are hope less. This now brings me to the second death.

The Second Death.

This term is mainly used in the book of Revelation, and mainly relates to the Christian faith. I know that some other people have their own spiritual beliefs, and I don't want to impose my faith on anybody nor be judgmental of anybody's spiritual beliefs. I am just living my faith loud and clear. I respect and appreciate that other people's opinions might differ, and that is fair enough. However as part of the human race, I am totally against anybody that inflicts harm or pain on a fellow human being both physically and spiritually.

There was a time, I wondered whether there are other ways to heaven?, and am happy that my life experience answered this question for me. Most of my life I have had to protect myself against people that practise dark magic (Witchcraft), and my help has only come from Lord, my experience has enabled me understand the power in the name of Jesus and the blood of Jesus. Prayers using His name have enabled me to overcome and continue to stand. In my opinion nothing else can break the power of, or protect a person the evil power of Witchcraft, than the name of Jesus.

Going back to the Second death, According to the Christian Faith, after the resurrection, then judgement, in which a soul / person goes to heaven or goes to hell which is the lake of fire for eternity. I know other faiths have similar concepts of the afterlife. However we have a common ground which is, everything we do in our lifetime is recorded, and in the Day of Judgment our life will be played back to us.

Bottom line it's the four letter word called Love that it all boils down too. The Lawyer asked Jesus, what to do to inherit external life, Jesus said what does it say in the Law, he said love God with all your heart, strength and Love, also love your neighbour as yourself.

Everybody has emotions, and we know, and we know what good emotions feel like and what negative and bad emotions feel like. Well Love is a good emotion and has the highest frequency on the emotional scale. The good feeling we experience from Love is what we want to spread and give to others always.

Finally doing to others, what we would like done back to us. These would hopefully be Love actions, and as we give it out it will come back to us. Also when we love God, we will not harm or hurt our fellow human beings. Remember everything we do is recorded.

REFERENCES

Ahmed, H. (2008) 'The Soul's Journey After Death in Islam'. Available at http://www.islamicinformation.net. 2008.
Accessed : 07/July 2016).

Aurelius, Marcus. *Meditations.* 2003

Barnes, J. Aristotle in Greek Philosophy. Oxford, 1999.

Bauer, C. Near Death Experience: The Truth Revealed. Indie Digital Publishing, 2010.

Biography.com. 'Socrates'.
http://www.biography.com/search/query/Socrates. 2016.
Jed McDonald (2012) 'Socrates and the Human Soul'
Available at http://www.cneuroscience.org
Accessed : 08 August 2016
Christian Neuroscience Society.

Cross, F. and E. Livingstone. *The Oxford Dictionary of the Church.* 1977.

Culter, Geoffrey John. *Is Reincarnation an Illusion?*

Hamilton, E., and H. Cairns, eds. *Socrates and the House Soul.* Princeton University Press, 1996.

'Have You Ever Thought about Your Eternity?'
http://www.eternityinyourheart.com. Accessed 20 May 2016.

Jewish Encyclopedia.com. 'Book of Wisdom: The Wisdom of Solomon'.

Jung, C. G. *Analytical Psychology: Its Theory and Practise.*

Korotkov,K.'SoulLeavingtheBodyPhoto'.http://www.metabung.org/deb un ked-soul-leaving-body-photo-russian.scientist-konstatin-korotov.T2447. Accessed 20 June 2016.

Newton, M. Journey of Souls. Llewellyn Publications, 2010.

'Philosophy of Religion'. http://www.Scandalon.co.uk.

Popper, K. R. *The Open Society and Its Enemies, Volume 1*. 1966.

Reynolds, H. Heaven through Pearly Gates. 2015.

'Somatic Death'. http://www.healthdrip.com. Assessed 19 May 2016.

'The Soul Journey from Death to Re-birth.' http://psychienergies.com/ articles interview_soul.html. Accessed 12 March 2016.

Steven, J., and S. Warwick-Smith. *The Michael Handbook*.

www.ingramcontent.com/pod-product-compliance
Lightning Source LLC
Chambersburg PA
CBHW050956050726
47592CB00007B/2594